Finding Significance at Home and Beyond...

Often we Christian mothers feel we must be "Supermom"—and that if we can't do it all, we don't measure up to society's or God's standards. That's why every Christian mother should read WHAT CAN A MOTHER DO? Judy Douglass will help you see the incredible value God has placed on you—right where you are! And in the pages of this book you'll find dozens of true examples and ideas to help you enjoy a significant ministry for Jesus Christ at home and beyond.

Ann Kiemel Anderson
Author, Speaker

Judy Downs Douglass goes beyond advice on "coping" with children, and shows creative ways to combine mothering and ministry. As the mother of two young children, I found the book inspiring, imaginative and very practical. I will use Judy's ideas to make my home more nurturing and my outreach more helpful.

Dale Hanson Bourke
Senior Editor
Today's Christian Woman

When the newborn infant crashes the big party of life, one person is all-important—Mommy. Her attitudes and actions set his lifetime course. What can she, and should she, do with this tiny piece of the next generation? The answers from Judy Douglass are practical, sensible and incredibly valuable—reaching right down to where Christian mothers are.

Jeanne Hendricks
Dallas, Texas

**Other Here's Life books by
Judy Downs Douglass**

He Loves Me

Single and Complete

What Can A Mother Do?

Judy Downs Douglass

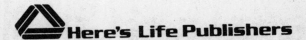
Here's Life Publishers

First Printing, April 1988

Published by
HERE'S LIFE PUBLISHERS, INC.
P. O. Box 1576
San Bernardino, CA 92402

HLP Product No. 952036
©1988, Judy Downs Douglass
All rights reserved.
Printed in the United States of America.

Library of Congress Cataloging-in-Publication Data
   Douglass, Judy Downs.
      What can a mother do? : finding significance at home and beyond / Judy
Downs Douglass.

      p.   cm.

      Bibliography: p.

      ISBN 0-89840-201-8 (pbk.) :

      1. Mothers—Religious life. 2. Douglass, Judy Downs. I. Title.
BV4529.D68 1988
248.8'431—dc 19   87-21753
CIP

Unless otherwise indicated, Scripture quotations are from the *Holy Bible, New
International Version,* ©1978 by the New York International Bible Society,
published by the Zondervan Corporation, Grand Rapids, Michigan.

Scripture quotations designated TLB are from *The Living Bible,* ©1971, Tyndale House Publishers, Wheaton, Illinois.

For More Information, Write:
   L.I.F.E. – P.O. Box A399, Sydney South 2000, Australia
   Campus Crusade for Christ – Box 300, Vancouver, B.C. V6C 2X3, Canada
   Campus Crusade for Christ – Pearl Assurance House, 4 Temple Row, Birmingham, B2 5HG, England
   Lay Institute for Evangelism – P.O. Box 8786, Auckland 3, New Zealand
   Campus Crusade for Christ – P.O. Box 240, Colombo Court Post Office, Singapore 9117
   Great Commission Movement of Nigeria – P.O. Box 500, Jos, Plateau State Nigeria, West Africa
   Campus Crusade for Christ International – Arrowhead Springs, San Bernardino, CA 92414, U.S.A.

Contents

Acknowledgments

DEDICATION

To Debbie and Michelle

This book is the product of six years of work on my part and of the help and contributions from hundreds of others. I am grateful to:

Debbie and Michelle, for making me a mother and helping me to discover God's just right plans for me in mothering and ministry.

My husband, Steve, for his constant love for me, belief in me and encouragement to me.

Cindy Peach, for invaluable assistance in research, transcribing, word processing, finalizing and every other detail of completing a manuscript.

Chris Kauffman, for her research and secretarial help in the early stages.

Grandma Gladys Douglass, for keeping the children joyfully during my writing getaways.

Sharon Lohman and other workers at Campus Crusade Child Care, for loving and caring for Debbie and Michelle when I needed to research or interview or write or edit.

All the moms who filled out surveys, answered questions, allowed me to interview them, attended my classes and in many other ways provided real-life examples of finding God's balance for ministry at home and beyond.

Barbie Harrison, Pamela Heim, Laurie Killingsworth, Janet Kobobel, Nancy Ortberg, Gayle Roper and Linda Wright, for their evaluations, insights and suggestions on my manuscript.

Dan Benson, Jean Bryant, Terry Smith, Barb Sherrill, Bob Dykstra and Karla Lenderink of Here's Life Publishers, for their hard work in bringing this book to reality.

Introduction

I have always loved schedules and deadlines. As a magazine writer and editor I reveled in plans and order and everything happening on time. When I became pregnant with my first child, it occurred to me that I might have to learn to be a little more flexible — but just how flexible I had no idea.

When Debbie was born, she was beautiful, perfect, delightful. But she had colic. Not the few-hours-in-the-evening kind of colic — the 24-hours-a-day kind. Her tummy always hurt, and she cried and cried and cried. Also, Debbie didn't need much sleep. I read that in time a baby would cut back to fourteen to sixteen hours of sleep a day. I marveled that a child would ever sleep fourteen to sixteen hours a day. Debbie rarely totaled more than nine or ten.

Debbie also had a very active mind and, of course, her new little body could do nothing to entertain her mind. I used toys, rattles, pictures, songs, dances — anything to keep her from crying. We walked, we rode, we swung.

I probably cried more during those first few months of Debbie's life than during the rest of my life put together. I was sure I would never feel rested again. I would never be able to put make-up on and get dressed all at one time. I would never look slim again. And I would never be able to do anything according to my schedule. Now, another child and several years later, life is somewhat more ordered, and structured more according to my own schedule, but along with the daily joys there are still the daily demands of young children.

For some people mothering seems to come naturally, but for me it is the most difficult assignment I've ever had. I'm committed to it, though. I'm certain that God called me to be the mother of Debbie and Michelle, and I will do the best job, in His power, that I possibly can.

One area in which I have felt particularly needy is that of balancing the priority of my family with my desire to make a significant contribution in my world. When I have a need, I usually look for solutions, so I began to talk to others. During the past several years I have talked to, surveyed, or interviewed more than 150 moms from around the world. Many of them have been in the midst of small children. Others were looking back and remembering. Some of them are in Christian work. Most are not. Some have been single moms. Some have chosen to school their children at home. Each has been trying to achieve that just-right-for-her balance between caring for her husband and her children, and developing as a significant person herself, reaching out beyond her family.

In this book I've tried to pull together some of their wisdom, their examples and their ideas in order to help other moms in the very significant task to which God has called us. My intention is to encourage you. I do not want you to be overwhelmed by the many possibilities presented—rather, my desire is that the stories of these mothers will motivate you and give you hope.

No one person could carry out even a small fraction of all the ideas shared here. My prayer is that, as you see how God uses other mothers, you will rejoice for the caring, for the lives being touched, for the growth in the Kingdom of God. And I pray that just once or twice God will speak to you and say, "This is something you can do."

1
Lost:
A Sense of
Personal Significance

My daughters, Debbie and Michelle, placed the array of angels on our table—two bright silver ones, a shiny brass angel, a lovely ceramic bell—while Steve lighted the elegant angel candle. I dished up peach cobbler for each of us. We were preparing to "celebrate with the angels."

"Yesterday Mom spoke to a group of women about Jesus," my husband Steve began. "Three of them said they wanted to invite Jesus into their lives as their Savior."

"You had a part in those women receiving Christ," I reminded the girls, "because you allowed me to go and share with them and because you prayed that God would use me in a special way. Now there are three new children in the family of God."

"What are the angels doing?" Steve asked.

"They're having a party!" Michelle exclaimed.

"They are celebrating because people asked Jesus into their heart!" Debbie added.

All four of us prayed, thanking God for the privilege of helping introduce people to Christ, thanking Him for these new sisters in the Lord, and praying for them as they began their new lives in Christ. Then we ate our cobbler.

A Significant Contribution

The "celebrate with the angels" party has become a cherished tradition in our home every time one of us is involved in the birth of a new believer. Every time we do that, God reminds us of the incredible privilege it is to tell people about His love. At that time I feel very significant. I feel that every little thing I do is important. But I haven't always felt that way. I particularly remember a conference one summer evening several years ago.

"The hour is urgent," the speaker was saying. "The world needs the Lord Jesus Christ. The world is hungry for God. This is no time for business as usual. Our lives must be supernatural. We must be spiritual revolutionaries."

"Sure," I thought to myself. "When will I ever do anything significant for the Lord again?"

When I was eight years old I had decided I wanted to become a writer. When I received Christ at the age of fifteen I had a definite sense that God had something special He wanted me to do. How thrilled I was that what He wanted me to do was write and edit for Him. For fourteen years I had the privilege of working in the Publications Department of Campus Crusade for Christ, writing and editing—to touch lives for Christ. I had seen God do wonderful things in my life and through my life. I felt very much as though I were living a supernatural life, as though I were making a significant contribution to the cause of Christ.

But now I had a very active fourteen-month-old. Just maintaining daily life overwhelmed me. And I was pregnant. When would I ever find the time to reach out and minister even to one other person, much less to do anything truly significant or satisfying?

Criteria for Self-Worth

I found myself in something of a crisis stemming from two distinct pressures in my life. The first had to do with a diminished sense of significance or self-worth, a common response to the demands of mothering. Recently I talked with a group of other young mothers who shared some of their struggles in this arena. Here are some of their responses:

> Colleen: The time involved in taking care of the children is so great that I feel like I lose myself; I lose "who I am."

> Kathy: Being at home with my two preschool children, in spite of all the pleasure and satisfaction it brings, is difficult for the simple reason that it is all-consuming. All of my time belongs to them — none of it to me. This seems to me a radical sacrifice.

> Sherry: When I became a mother I felt that I lost my identity as a person. My husband still went to work and had his activities, but my whole life was different. Sitting at home, feeding, changing and entertaining my baby, did not fulfill my need to be acknowledged for having done a good job.

Psychologist Bruce Narramore tells us that most psychologists agree on which basic conditions in life contribute to our sense of feeling significant or of value.[1]

The five most important criteria for personal worth and significance include:

1. *Security.* We need to know that we are secure, that we are safe. This often involves financial as well as physical security. For many people, "what I have" defines security.

2. *Confidence.* It's important that we feel we have life basically under control. We want to know we're special, and that we can do something of value. "What I can do" contributes to our feeling of confidence.

3. *A sense of belonging.* For all of history the family unit has provided a sense of belonging. That is often not the case today. We sometimes seek to find that "I am a part

of something" feeling by joining groups and participating in various activities.

4. *A sense of being loved.* Loving relationships are a cornerstone for a healthy and happy life. Finding out "who loves me" is a driving quest in the lives of many, adults and children both.

5. *Purpose.* Each of us wants to feel that we have something to contribute to the world. We want to know we have accomplished something of value. We want the answer to "Why am I here?"

In my career I had experienced a sense of personal worth in all of these areas. I felt secure in my job, primarily because I was sure I was doing what God had called me to do.

I had confidence. I had been doing my work long enough to feel I was doing a good job and was comfortable with it.

I definitely had a sense of belonging. My co-workers and I were very close and had an excellent working relationship.

I felt loved by those I worked with as well as by my husband and other important people in my life.

And the assurance that my writing and editing touched lives for the Lord gave a tremendous sense of purpose to my life.

Diminished Sense of Value

My new role of motherhood, however, gave me very little assurance of value in any of these areas.

Security. I had a sense of security in my job. There was no one else to do it, though there were times I felt like giving the responsibility to someone else. I often did not feel sure of my health or my sanity. But in motherhood my "just surviving" mentality hardly gave me a sense of real security.

Confidence. I did not find mothering easy and I had almost no confidence that I was doing an adequate job. I read a lot of books, and sometimes they helped, but too often they caused me to feel inferior or that I was a failure.

Belonging. Yes, there was a sense that I belonged to this child. But I had very little opportunity to belong anywhere else. I often missed the camaraderie of the office.

Being loved. I was still certain of my husband's love, though I didn't feel lovely very often. As for my wonderful little daughter, she generally made demands rather than returning love to me.

Purpose. I knew that what I was doing in Debbie's life had great, long-term significance and purpose. Because there was little tangible evidence of results in those early days, though, it was hard to recognize any purpose.

Conflicting Priorities

My other area of crisis came from the conflicting messages I seemed to be receiving about my use of time. On one hand, some of my friends pointed out that now that I was a mother, my ministry would be to my family. My children would be my field of evangelism, my primary disciples, the focus of my life. I wouldn't be able to do much else if I wanted to do a good job with my children.

On the other hand, people reminded me that God had given me certain skills and that I must continue to use them in His service. These people stressed the importance of my finding personal fulfillment in feeling useful. After all, if I was not happy and fulfilled, my children wouldn't be happy either. They urged me not to stifle my children, but to give them the variety of experience and exposure that my career and ministry would provide.

It seemed it had to be one extreme or the other, but I couldn't believe that. *There must be a balance—where is it?*

I was not the only one who experienced these stresses. I talked with many mothers who were struggling with the same things. They all were asking, just as I was, "What can a mother do?"

2
Found:
An Assurance of
Personal Significance

Fortunately, God did not leave me hanging in a closet of frustration and insignificance. Nor did He allow me to shut myself away from the opportunities He had for me. Through study of His Word, extensive conversations with my husband, and the counsel of godly mothers, I began to get God's perspective on my life as a mother.

First, He dealt with my feeling that I had lost any sense of significance in my life. He reminded me that He, and He alone, was the source of my sense of personal value and worth and significance.

He reminded me that He loved me unconditionally (Romans 5:8), eternally (Jeremiah 31:3), and sacrificially (John 15:13).

He reminded me that my security had to be in Him, and that in Him I was truly safe. Jesus said, "No one can snatch [my sheep] out of my hand" (John 10:27,28).

He reminded me that in Him—and only in Him—I can have confidence. I am a special person, created in God's image (Genesis 1:26,27). I am the crown of creation (Psalm 8:4,5). I am capable of great accomplishments (Philippians 4:13). God is my source of and reason for confidence.

God reminded me that I belong in the greatest group of

all — His own family. He adopted me and made me His own child (Ephesians 1:4-6; John 1:12).

Then He reminded me that I have a significant purpose. His primary purpose in my life is to make me like Jesus (Romans 8:28,29a). As I become more and more like Christ, I will fulfill His purpose for me by reflecting the glory of God (1 Peter 2:9).

God has other specific purposes for my life as well. One is to bear *good fruit:* "You did not choose Me, but I chose you, and appointed you, that you should go and bear fruit, and that your fruit should remain" (John 15:16). Also God has prepared *good works* for me: "For we are God's workmanship, created in Christ Jesus to do good works which God prepared in advance for us to do" (Ephesians 2:10). In the parable of the talents (Matthew 25:14-30) Christ tells us that we are to be *good stewards* of all that He gives us in life.

Source of Significance

As I understood all that I have because I have Jesus, I began to recognize that it was not meeting all these important criteria in my life — in my career and ministry, or as a mother — that brought fulfillment. Rather it arose out of my relationship with God through Jesus Christ. He alone could give me the love, security, confidence, sense of belonging and purpose for my life that I needed.

My friend, Barbie Harrison, mother of three, adds her thoughts:

> I am increasingly convinced that women today equate their value too closely with what they do rather than who they are. We want to be able to measure our accomplishments and see our achievements. My ministry should not fulfill my need to be needed, though that may come as a side benefit; rather, it should flow from my deep love for the Lord. Being deep in Him will result in deep ministry. I constantly struggle with the balance between doing and being, resting in the Lord and serving Him. However, I

know there is a direct correlation between my thirst for
the Lord and my "success" in ministry. Ministry is always a result of who I am, not just what I can do.

Defining Ministry

Thus, over time, God restored my sense of significance,
unrelated to my mothering or any ministry I might have.
But what about ministry? Was it possible for me to do jus-
tice to my family responsibilities and still be involved in
ministry? Could God really use me?

Yes, undoubtedly. Let me share some fresh definitions
I have discovered that have both encouraged and freed me.

I want to live a supernatural life—but what does that
mean? I believe, very simply, it means to walk closely with
God in the power of His Spirit. It means to be totally available to God, to be the person He wants me to be and to do
what He wants me to do. I can do that anytime or anywhere,
whether it's sharing Christ with someone, or writing an ar-
ticle, or making cookies with my children, or doing the
laundry.

Undoubtedly the hardest place for me to live super-
naturally is at home. There life is so repetitious. The chores
seem endless. My husband has needs. The children have
needs. Yet, as I allow God to control me and empower me
and live His life through me, I am living a supernatural life.

What does it mean to have a ministry? What is ministry?

In her book *How to Grow a Women's Minis-tree,* Daisy
Hepburn quotes a definition of ministry as "any relationship in which both parties benefit."

Steve says that four elements will usually be found in
true ministry:

1. The parties: God, you and others.
2. A service or help of some kind.
3. A purpose of glorifying God and drawing people closer

to Him.

4. The power of the Holy Spirit versus the power of the flesh.

This could be summarized: God, by His Spirit, works through you to serve or help another person, glorifying Himself and drawing you both closer to Him.

How would I define ministry? Certainly, ministry includes the obvious such as evangelism and discipleship. We are commanded in Scripture to seek those who might not know Christ and tell them how they can receive Him and become God's children. We are admonished also to help believers grow and mature and become true disciples who will reach out to others.

Ministry is serving. I believe it begins with an attitude of selflessness, of willingness to give of myself. Jesus told us that He came not to be served, but to serve. As He served, so are we to go out and serve others (John 13). In essence, ministry is being available to God to step into opportunities and touch lives for Him.

Ministry is a choice. When those opportunities come, we decide whether or not we will step into them. We can choose to avoid them—I have done that sometimes when serving has seemed inconvenient or too demanding or too tiring. Or we can choose to be available to God to care, to love, to serve.

Arenas of Opportunity

As a mother I have two primary arenas of ministry. The first, the priority, is my family, and that's what we will consider first. The second arena of ministry—beyond our families—we will examine beginning in chapter 6.

If ministry means to be available to God to care, to love, to serve, to step into opportunities to touch lives, I have a ministry every day with my family.

Certainly our children, and sometimes our husbands, will be our primary field of evangelism. What an opportunity, what a privilege to be the one to introduce the man we love or the wonderful little ones that God has given us to our Lord. What a treasure!

The family is equally a place of discipleship. Our children indeed are our primary disciples. Serving could easily be defined by the word "mother." How special to be able to follow our Lord's example in selfless giving of ourselves for our children day after day. We have the opportunity to teach them God's truths, to provide them an environment in which they'll experience God's love and learn what it means to live for God. We can guide them, help them make decisions and lead them into full, responsible maturity in Christ.

Opportunities to serve our families never cease. My husband must be my first priority after my relationship with God. I want to be a partner with him, to do all I can to help him be and do all God has for him. I want to encourage him, challenge and comfort him, and meet any needs I can.

Many other mothers also see their families as just this priority ministry that God has given them:

Donna Lynn: Peter tells us, "Tend the flock that is in your charge, not by constraint, but willingly, not for shameful gain but eagerly, not as domineering over those in your charge but being examples to the flock" (1 Peter 5:2-4). I regard my family as my flock.

Coryne: My home is my primary ministry in terms of priority and time. Being a helpmate to my husband — encouraging, listening, sharing ideas, assisting him, praying for him — strengthens his ministry. My children are my key disciples — I minister by teaching, being available, listening, knowing them so well I sense when they are hurting or have special needs.

Pamela: Once a person makes certain commitments, she forever limits her subsequent choices. Having decided to be a wife and a mother, I am morally bound to make all other decisions in light of that.

Carolyn: My family is my priority ministry — to allow and assist my husband to reach his potential in serving Christ, and to see my children mature into men and women of godly character who desire to serve Christ.

My significance as a person must always come from my relationship with God. Yet God gives me an incredibly significant ministry as a mother.

3
Significance in Mothering

Is being a mother really, truly, an important job?

Are you really the best person to care for your child? Aren't there professionals trained in child development who would do a better job than some inexperienced mother? Do you cringe if someone asks, "What do you do?" and you have to say, "I'm just a housewife" or "I don't work"? Isn't it better for your children to learn independence than to be so dependent on Mom?

These are the kinds of questions we hear today. Do they reflect reality? Or is it still true that the hand that rocks the cradle rules the world?

I believe mothering is possibly the most meaningful responsibility there is.

Significance for Mom

The greatest significance that mothering has for me lies in the fact that I have the opportunity to build a human being.

Some entire professions are dedicated to helping people. Physicians, psychologists, teachers and child care workers are a few of those who commit much of their lives to the care and development of human beings, and especially the young. Sometimes the impact of people in these professions on a single person is great, but most often it is diluted by the demands of so many to be cared for.

In contrast, I have the privilege, as a mother, of performing all those valuable functions with great impact on a single life. I help that little person grow into a big, mature person, one who can handle life and have something to contribute to others. I am thus making a lasting contribution to another life as well as to future generations.

So often when we look for a place to accomplish something and to contribute to life, we look for immediate rewards and gratifications. Although there are tangible, immediate rewards in childrearing — not the least of which are lots of hugs and kisses — the primary, most important ones, are long term. Most of those results will not be seen until much later in our lifetime, but to me they will certainly be of great value.

The spiritual contributions I can make and the opportunities I have to disciple my children, to build into their lives a love for God and an understanding of how to walk with Him, are extremely important. I have a continuing chance for long-term, in-depth, live-it-out discipleship.

Kim expresses a similar thought: I feel very responsible, along with my husband and God, for how these children turn out. I am with them most of the time; therefore my actions and attitudes are what they see the most. It is a tremendous responsibility that I don't feel up to sometimes.

Another vital benefit and evidence of the significance of mothering has been my own personal growth. More than anything in the world, I desire to be the person that God created me to be, to become more like the Lord Jesus. No other experience in my life has had such an impact on me — to make me more like Jesus — as that of being a mother.

I thought I knew how to walk with God in difficult circumstances. I thought I knew how to grow in my Christian life. I thought I was becoming more like Jesus each day. At work and in other adult relationships it hadn't been too difficult to control my emotional responses, even in trying situations. I was usually able to act appropriately.

Having children, however, has given me opportunities to see my strengths and weaknesses better. Those first few months with my crying baby were especially revealing. I cried constantly, too. I was depressed, sometimes angry. Yet God gently reminded me of two important facts.

First, I was just right for Debbie. I was the one God had chosen to love her, comfort her, give her a sense of security, and help her grow into the person God created her to be.

Second, Debbie was just right for me. She was the one God chose to use to reveal my weaknesses, to help me see where I needed to grow, to contribute to my spiritual development and maturity in my walk with God.

Other mothers have shared some of my thoughts on the significance of mothering for Mom herself.

> Julie: I think about how rewarding it is to have such great influence on a young life. You can make a child almost anything, you know. That's a big responsibility, and it makes me feel really important. There is nothing that I'd rather be doing.

> Kathy: It's a job, too, you know. I am not just a homemaker. It is rewarding, and I feel like I am accomplishing something, just as if I went to work and accomplished things.

> Betty: Sometimes it's hard to put yourself last and put others in front of you. I guess that's where the real commitment comes in. It is purposeful, and it is a real accomplishment even though it's hard to see the end result.

Significance for My Children

The next area of significance in my being a mother is for my children. Dr. Jack Raskin, a child psychiatrist at Children's Orthopedic Hospital at the University of Washington in Seattle, believes that the key to healthy personality development lies in the "child's close, unbroken attachment in the early months to people who care for him. Too much disruption of this imbeds in the personality traits that can be destructive for a lifetime."[1]

Dr. Urie Bronfenbrenner, professor of human development at Cornell University, adds that the child needs someone who will not pack up and go home at 5:00. This caretaker must love the child more than other people's children and the child must return the love. Or to put it another way, "The child should spend a substantial amount of time with someone who's crazy about him."[2] As Brenda Hunter points out in *Where Have All The Mothers Gone?* this caretaker sounds suspiciously like a mother.[3]

Burton White in *The First Three Years Of Life* agrees. He stresses the importance of the person who spends the most time with the young child, the primary caretaker. He indicates that this person will, more than any other, influence the child's view of himself and of his world.[4]

Personally, I want to be that person for my daughters. I know what values are important to me, and I want to pass them on to my children. I care that my children have a great sense of being loved unconditionally, that they have security, that they have a sense of belonging, that they have confidence in themselves and in God and that they learn the purpose for which God created them. These are the things we talked about earlier that help us feel significant, and I want them for my children as well. It is essential, however, to remember that it is God who will provide what our children need. When we fail or when because of circumstances we are unable to be that primary caretaker, God will take care of our children. He can take our love, our commitment and our good intentions, as well as our failures and inadequacies, and work them for good for us and for our children as we depend on Him.

I also want my children to know Christ. I want them to grow spiritually, to be like Him, to trust Him, to choose Him above all others in their lives, and to be or do all that

God has for them. I want them to grow physically, to be active, to be skilled. I want them to grow mentally, to be stimulated, to be creative. I want them to grow socially, to be responsible adults, to know how to relate to people. I want them to be mature, caring people. I want them to be prepared to lead in the world.

> Stacy: Lately I've been faced with the awesome fact that teaching our kids is a never-ending job. We not only have to feed and clothe and love them, but we also have to teach them in everyday circumstances how to deal with life—mainly by our example. This is an awesome responsibility, not to be taken lightly.

> Erin: It's very hard for me, in the day-to-day routine of my life, to remember that I am raising people. Although they are only five and one, these people deserve my patience and my consideration—which I would give to any friend or acquaintance—simply because they are human beings.

> Teri: The hardest thing about being a mother is knowing how to rise above my own inadequacy, and knowing how to understand and guide my children through life. I hope I'm equipping them for the future God has for them.

Certainly, I feel inadequate to convey all of these things to my children. I will fail—far too often. I know there are others who have much greater mothering skills than I have, yet I am sure no one else is as committed to instilling these values into my children as I am. Of course, I will get help from others, both informally and formally, but I truly believe that someone who spends a great deal of time with my children is going to have a significant impact on their lives. I want that significant impact to be the right one. We will look later at a whole chapter on ways to do that.

Significance for Our World

Finally, my mothering is greatly significant for our world. There is in the world today a tremendous vacuum of spiritual and moral values and of character. There cer-

tainly is also a lack of leadership and responsible citizen-
ship.

Herbert Orral, an educator for thirty-three years,
states:

> Kids today are searching for something to live for, but
> they are having a tremendous struggle finding answers.
> We no longer have the support structures in the cultures
> that existed when I was growing up. How many families
> in this area or in the country have a strong church affilia-
> tion? No longer does the family look to the local church
> for support, and the immediate family is failing to
> provide youth with the emotional support needed.
>
> Many of my students go home daily to empty houses.
> Home is little more than a bedroom and a place to hang
> their clothes. Where are the parents? It is hard to do your
> own thing and raise children well.[5]

Norman Almond, a high school guidance counselor, has
worked with students for more than fourteen years. He
states, "Kids who come to my office reveal an emptiness in
their lives. A lack of love, a lack of spiritual values, a lack
of discipline. That old security is gone."[6]

As we present a loving, disciplined home and family, we
will stand out in our neighborhoods. We can demonstrate
to the world that it is possible to provide an atmosphere of
acceptance and security for our children. We can model the
kind of home that people truly desire in their hearts.

We also can uphold moral and spiritual standards that
allow people to develop fully and to relate with each other
in lovingkindness. We can rear children who will pass these
values on to their children.

My mothering provides a model of its importance at a
time when many are seeking to diminish its significance. It
is ironic that, in the current emphasis on self actualization,
many mothers are abandoning the most fulfilling contribution they can make in life. Mothering helps to produce the
children who will grow into capable adults, able to live by

high spiritual and moral standards. Those children who grow up in the security of love and affirmation will be equipped to lead our world in the next generation.

A mother named Betty says: Our example of the things we build into our home, and the things we have brought to our home from when we were children, will enable our children to go out and build good life responses and be good citizens and good church workers.

Linda adds: I know the neighbors can see all that I am doing, the good and the bad. It's important that I be doing what I should, that I be a good model.

In *What Is a Family?* Edith Schaeffer states it so well:

But the basic resolve to consider the total relationship of husband and wife through the years and the total relationship of the family as an environment for growing new people, children, and grandchildren is more important than any one incident, more important than human words can express. Over and over again, someone in a relationship needs to consider the family as a career, a project, serious enough to be willing to be the one to "scramble up over jagged rocks to feed the birds, so that they won't become extinct." The family is even more important than rare species of birds, and taking on the career of being a mother and wife is a fabulously rare lifework in the twentieth century, and a very challenging job. A wasted effort? A thankless job? An undignified slave? No, a most exciting possibility of turning the tide, of saving the species, of affecting history, of doing something that will be felt and heard in ever-widening circles.[7]

Mothering is to me a highly significant job. It contributes tremendously to my life, to my own growth, and to my sense of value and purpose as I make a contribution to another life and to the world. It is significant to my children for how it enables them to grow into the persons God intends them to be. And it is certainly significant for my world as we model the kind of life that is possible in Christ and as we prepare the future generation for leadership.

4
Home: The Most Significant Place in the World

In Maurice Sendak's *Where The Wild Things Are,*[1] Max grows tired of being king of all the wild things, and he says, "I'm lonely. I want to go back. I want to go where I'm loved the most." He wanted to go home.

There are many important places in our lives.

School, for example. What we learn there takes us through the remainder of our lives. It's where we begin to learn to relate to people and where we often make life-long friends. Certainly it is where we spend a great deal of our time during childhood.

Church is also an important place. We go there to worship God within the body of Christ. There we are taught from the Word of God and have fellowship with other believers. We receive love and caring, and we have needs met. The church is often a channel through which we reach out and touch other lives.

As adults we put a great deal of our time, effort and energy into the work we do, contributing in that way to society. We often find satisfaction and a sense of achievement and growth at our workplace, and it gives us the means for providing for our family's needs.

As important as school, church and workplace are,

though, home — as Max discovered — is far more important. Home is the most significant place in the world for us and for our children.

Home Should Be . . .

Where you are loved the most. Though others in your life elsewhere will love you, consistent, unconditional love should always be available at home.

Where people know you the best. You should be able to be yourself there and know that you'll be accepted, supported and affirmed. Even as a baby, the feelings you had about yourself and about life came from the atmosphere of your home. Whether you think you're smart or not so smart, capable or incapable, attractive or not attractive depend largely on what you learned at home.

A growing place. Home should give you the freedom to experiment and develop as an individual, to find out what you're good at and what you're not so good at, to try and to fail. You need to be able to express freely, in any number of ways, the creativity that God has placed within you.

Where relationships are important. This is where people should learn to care about others and believe the best about each other. They should be available to each other in times of need, and should be able to enjoy each other.

A place of oneness. Despite differences or disagreements, everyone can say, "I'm for you and you're for me, and we're for each other. We are a family." Loyalty develops here. You learn that others in your family will be loyal to you, and you determine to be loyal to them.

A place of responsibility. Here a person learns how to live in this world, to fulfill obligations, and to be a good citizen.

A place of memories and traditions. We learn about our roots at home, and we establish traditions of our own that give us stability and a sense of permanence. All our lives, we carry memories of home and of all that our family has meant to us.

A place of shelter. It's so comforting to be able to come home when life has been difficult, when friends have been unkind, when success has been elusive, or when loving has been painful.

No home, of course, can be all of these things all the time, or even some of the time. No home will be perfect. Nevertheless, a home dedicated to God and filled with people seeking to please Him and to love each other has the potential to truly be the most significant place in the world to a person.

To Work or Not to Work

If mothering is a significant job and if home is the most important place in the world, then a woman's leaving the home and going out into the marketplace, especially when her children are young, must be evaluated carefully. Estimates are that 52 percent of mothers of preschoolers work outside the home at this time. Of course, that means 48 percent don't, and many of the 52 percent who do, work only part time. Still that's a much greater percentage of mothers who leave their young children for major portions of the day than has been true previously.

The question of whether or not to work outside the home, and how much, confronts us consistently now. The three primary reasons a mother with younger children would be working are:

1. It is a financial necessity.

2. It means a more comfortable standard of living.

3. A woman truly desires a career for personal satisfaction.

Financial Reasons

For many mothers there seems no alternative to full-time work outside the home if her family is to be fed, clothed

and sheltered. Yet some of these moms, as well as many of
those who work mainly to provide the extras for their
families, are reevaluating their situations. One of the first
things to consider is the comparison of real costs with the
benefits of full-time work. There are a number of major
costs incurred when a mother works outside the home. Tom
Allen, a pastor in Iowa, has run some representative figures
on what could happen to a woman's salary:

> A mother who earns $14,000 a year will have a month-
> ly gross income of $1,166.66. Her fixed expenses will run
> as follows:
> Federal income tax, 15 percent — $175
> State income tax, 3 percent — $35
> Social Security tax, 7 percent — $81.66
> Tithe, 10 percent — $117
> Transportation, 400 miles at 30 cents/mile — $120
>
> That's a total of $528.66 in fixed expenses, leaving her
> with $638 for discretionary spending.
>
> However, there are more expenses that will occur
> primarily because she is working. I have honed these
> down to what I believe are totally realistic expenditures.
> Notice:
>
> Lunches, $1.50/day — $30
> Restaurant, carry-out meals for rushed evenings or
> nights when she is too tired to cook — $40
> Extra clothes and dry cleaning — $50
> Forfeited saving on thrift shopping — $50
> Hairdresser — $20
> Employee Insurance — $15
> Daycare, one child, $50/week — $200
> I-owe-it-to-myself treats — $50
>
> Add up these expenditures for a total of $455. Added
> to the fixed expenses of $528.66, you have $983.66 worth
> of expenses that a working mother is paying out of her
> salary simply because she is working. That leaves her
> with $183, which is the true salary for her month's work.
> I think every mother who works needs to ask herself: "Is
> what I'm doing worth $45.75 a week?"[2]

Other Costs

For most moms there are additional costs that are not financial.

> Chris: It is so hard to find the balance between my home and my outside activities and job. I am constantly worrying about whether I am being to my girls all that they need me to be.

> Laurie: I'm never sure I'm giving enough time to each child since I am forced to work. I do not feel successful at my number one responsibility on this earth because I do not have the time to put into it.

Probably one of the most important costs is fatigue. I do not have a job outside my home, but I know that on the days when I am busy with my writing or speaking or other responsibilities, by evening I am so exhausted I want to rest. I'm not eager to fix a meal. I am not particularly interested in giving my children "quality time." I hope they will play happily by themselves so I can concentrate on restoring some energy.

Another cost is the need for organization at home. If the working mother is not well organized—as well as all other family members—there can be disorientation and disorder, if not outright chaos, in the home. And mother will seldom find the free time to do the things she really wants to do or needs to do for her own self.

Creative Alternatives

For those who feel the costs are too great, or who just want to explore other possibilities, there are many creative alternatives to working full time outside the home. One of the most obvious is to work in your home. In *A Complete Guide for the Working Mother,* Margaret Albrecht suggests, "If you feel strongly about mothering the children yourself, you are there to do it (when you work at home). There is no financial outlay for child care, or the other costs of an outside job, not even clothes. For some women the greatest appeal is 'I can be my own boss.' However, at home, work can result in the same need as any other job for organization or home management."[3]

Good Housekeeping's *101 Practical Ways to Make Money at Home* suggests:

> It's not necessary to have the makings of a woman tycoon to work successfully at home. What you do need, though, is considerable self-discipline, resourcefulness and the ability to maintain your initial enthusiasm for your project over long periods.
>
> You also need good health and plenty of energy since it takes stamina to do two jobs. And every wife and mother already has one.
>
> Third, it's absolutely critical that you make a realistic appraisal of your skills.[4]

The Small Business Administration suggests that anyone thinking of operating her own business should rate herself objectively on the following ten traits: initiative, attitude toward others, leadership, responsibility, organizing ability, industry, decisions, sincerity, perseverance and physical energy. In choosing a home business you should consider your skills, your experience and background, your time and facilities, your goals, the market.[5]

The list of ideas for your own business is endless. Let me list just a few that some of the many books on this subject suggest: mail order sales, catering, baking, box lunches, food gifts, party cooking, alterations and mending, custom-made clothing, custom-made home furnishings, doll clothing, raising plants for sale, growing herbs, plant and garden center, landscaping, secretarial service, bookkeeping and accounting, addressing service, telephone answering service, clipping service, translation, children's birthday parties, entertainment bureau, baby sitting, after-school child care, grooming salon for dogs, dog walking, animal sitting, breeding animals, flower arranging lessons, cooking classes, sewing classes, needlework classes, language lessons, music lessons, tutoring, natural childbirth classes, handicrafts, needlework, picture framing, interior decorating, photography, fix-it services, furniture refinishing, telephone selling, party selling, birthday cakes for college kids, writing fillers for newspapers and magazines, writing greeting cards.

For many, an alternative to full-time work would be part-time work. Many of the businesses just listed would be appropriate also for part-time work. In addition, substitute teaching and many other jobs such as museum tours, clerking, sales, and fast food service offer part-time employment. Thus, you can manage your hours so you're away from your children as little as possible.

Brenda Hunter, a single mother of two young children, tells of arranging her life so she was able to support her children, without being away from them, through a part-time business of her own run from her home. Another possibility includes combining with a teenager so that you work in the morning and the teenager works in the afternoon to fulfill one job. If the purpose for working is to provide extras or lessons or opportunities for your children, you might consider an increasingly popular approach: bartering. You trade a skill you have, perhaps sewing, for a need you have, say, piano lessons.

With wisdom from God and creative alternatives, it is often possible for a mother not to have to be away from her child full time in order to meet financial needs.

Personal Satisfaction

But what if the reason for working is not financial? What if it is primarily for personal satisfaction? I can certainly identify with this. After fourteen years in a career as a writer and editor, my decision to stay home and be a mother was not an easy one to make, nor has it always been easy to live with. But I believe it is right for me. I believe God has given me this priority for this particular time in my life.

As I've indicated, I feel that mothering is extremely sig-

nificant. I have committed myself to giving my children the
best possible opportunities to be and do all that God wants
for them. I am grateful that I can be at home with my
daughters and still occasionally be involved in writing and
speaking, my two primary professional interests. I have
been able to continue developing my skills — and I feel I am
making a significant contribution with those skills.

Let me suggest a few ideas from which you could choose.
One approach is to be involved part time in your chosen
profession. Perhaps you are a teacher and could do substitute teaching in order to maintain that, or perhaps you
could teach on a short-term or part-time basis. Perhaps
yours is a talent that could be used on a special project from
time to time.

Another approach might be to utilize your skill at home.
If you have accounting abilities, you could run a small accounting business from your home. It is important to me
to maintain my abilities and my skills, but possibly all I
need to do is keep my fingers in the pot with a part-time or
occasional opportunity.

Perhaps your profession does not lend itself to part-
time or occasional work. You might consider volunteering
in some civic or Christian organization that has a need for
your skills. I believe one of the greatest fallacies that has
been swallowed by American women today is that what you
earn makes what you do valuable. Work itself is valuable.
Your contribution to society further enhances its value. To
volunteer your time and skills to serve others is of great
worth. And if the service you provide helps to further God's
kingdom, how much better. Of course, volunteering is not
necessarily better than being paid, but if you desire to give
priority to your family and at the same time be a good
steward of the talents and gifts God has given you, volunteering can be a more viable option than a full-time job.

Another approach would be to look for ministry opportunities rather than a job. A person with people skills could

be very effective in reaching out to others in the name of our Lord. Much of the rest of this book is devoted to ideas for doing just that.

Some working moms have found it not only desirable but enjoyable to return home. Linguist Deborah Fallows, author of *A Mother's Work,* decided to stay home because "I think parents have a special place in child rearing. A child gets more consistent attention and love of a very different nature from a parent than from anybody else." She indicates that "a feeling that is left over from the early women's movement is that full-time parenthood has to be boring and involve a lot of drudgery and make you go bananas. But that doesn't have to be the case. Professional women can find other outlets for their skills." For those without professional or academic training she says, "I think it would be just as interesting to be at home with kids and volunteer to work for the school board a few hours a day as it would to be on an assembly line."[6]

There are mothers who seem to be able to do it all. They work full-time outside the home, maintain their own spiritual life, care for husband and home, and rear well-adjusted, godly children. That ability and flexibility are real gifts from God.

Home Working

Mary Pride, a former radical feminist, challenges us to some new thoughts concerning "home working" in her book *The Way Home:*

> To call only women who leave the home working wives amounts to saying that women who stay home don't work. This psychological word game is at the root of our modern career movement.
>
> Careerism is based on an inferiority complex as follows: (1) Only men's work has worth; women's traditional work is useless; therefore, (2) I must get a job to prove I am somebody. If all the action is out in the men's economic opportunity sphere, well then, we all

have to crowd into that end of the bus.

But 'tis not so, not so at all.

Homeworking . . . is the center of the passage in Titus that tells young wives how to live a Christian life. Homeworking is what young wives are supposed to do. Homeworking is a job.[7]

When women were stuck at home in the '50s with only their birth control pills and dishwashers for company, no wonder they went crazy. If God really wanted us to live that way, we could swallow our frustrations and do it, but since it was an abnormal lifestyle, frustration led to rebellion. When people abandon God's way, eventually their lifestyle collapses. Barrenness and idleness are no substitutes for fruitfulness and productivity. The answer—not home-abandoning careerism but home business.[8]

You are significant as a mom. Your job is important. Your home is the most important place in the world—a growing place for human beings. These facts should weigh heavily in all your decisions relative to your use of time and your direction in life.

5
Significance for Your Children

How many times have you desired that magical, storybook promise of three wishes? If you could wish for your children anything at all as an inheritance, what three things might you wish for them?

I wish many different things for my children—happiness, health, a good marriage, success, fulfillment. I want them to be good people. But I think I can sum it all up in three wishes. If they are to make the most of their lives, they need first, a personal relationship with God; second, a good character; and third, a useful life.

A Relationship With God

Nothing is more important in any person's life than establishing a relationship with God, coming to know Him personally through His Son Jesus Christ. He gives us the assurance of forgiveness of sins, eternal life, and the power to live the kind of life for which He has created us. He alone can give our children the things that will make them know their worth—security, a sense of belonging, a valid confidence, unconditional love and a purpose in life.

A relationship with God and an understanding of how to walk in the power of the Spirit assure our children access to all the fruit of the Spirit in their daily lives: love, joy, peace, patience, kindness, goodness, gentleness, faithfulness, and self-control. These contribute to the full and abundant life that God provides, and to good health as well.

A relationship with the loving creator God of the universe gives us the strength, the faith, the perseverance to go on in the difficult trials that come to everyone's life.

When our children have a relationship with God, we know that He is always with them even when we can't be — on that first day of school, when they spend the night at a friend's, as they travel to another city to play baseball, or on that first date. All the things that seem to give stability to their lives may disappear, but God will always be there to guide them, to protect them, to empower them.

How can we help our children establish that relationship with God? Since this is the most important thing we could give them as an inheritance, let's use an acrostic with the word **MOST** to consider some how-to's.

Model

Observe

Support

Train

MODEL

We must provide a model of the Christian life. Our walk with God should be so vibrant, so real, so enjoyable that our children will see it and desire it. Being a Christian must not be perceived as simply a lot of rules, a Sunday activity, or an occasional moral guide in our lives. We must demonstrate that Christ is relevant to every area of our lives. Our children should see us talking to Him and about Him. When we explode in anger, they need to hear us ask forgiveness from them and from God. They must know that He gives joy and peace in the most difficult circumstances — in the devastation of failure, for example, or in the disappointment of hurtful friends, or in the despair of losing a loved one. They need to realize that God provides the power to become all that He created us to be.

OBSERVE

We must observe our children day by day, looking for opportunities to show them how a relationship with God can be a part of their daily lives. When they are fearful, our family reads Psalm 23 together. When they get excited about David and Goliath, we talk about trusting God when something is too big for us. When they discover us in tears, we tell of our hurt and of God's comfort. All these things help them see a relationship with God as vital to our lives.

SUPPORT

We need to provide an environment that creates in our children a hunger for God, and we need to assure them that their search for and questioning of Him will be respected. As they come to know Him intimately, they will grow to love Him, and as they love Him, they will be willing to obey Him—and that is the most essential thing: to obey God. If this is to happen in their lives, they need to see us working out our relationship with God in our daily living. They need to know that we will listen to them, answer their questions, pray with them, and support them.

TRAIN

As important as living out the Christian life before our children is, it is not enough. We must also teach them what it is we have, and how they can have it, too. Deuteronomy 6:6-9 tells us we are to teach our children through every event of life. As we sit, as we stand, as we walk, wherever we go, whatever we're doing, we should be teaching them about God and what He can and should mean to them.

And of course, we must tell them how they can know Jesus Christ.

One of the things we do in our family is celebrate spiritual birthdays—the day of our second birth. This reminds us of what God has done for us, and it gives us an opportunity to share how we received Christ.

One of the greatest joys in my life came the day Debbie invited Christ into her life. We had been doing many of these things I've mentioned—we had prayed for her, included her in many spiritual activities, and read numerous Bible stories to her. We also had told her about receiving Christ and about others who had received Christ.

Then one day she found a copy of the "Good News Glove," a comic book presentation of the gospel, and she asked me to read it to her. As we read it through she seemed to understand the truths clearly. We spent a great deal of time discussing the meaning of sin and our need for a Savior and for forgiveness. She indicated very firmly and sincerely that she wanted to invite Christ into her life and to know that she would be forgiven of her sins. I am delighted to say that there were immediate results in Debbie's life. The most obvious was her strong new desire to be good.

Equally joyful was the day Michelle received Christ as her Savior. She and Debbie and I had talked quite a bit about having Jesus in your heart and had read through the "Good News Glove" several times. This day she was ready.

But helping them receive Christ is just the beginning. Then we have a responsibility to guide our children as they grow into maturity. Many of the things that we have done to lead them to initiate a relationship with God will be the means for their growth as well. Primarily we need to model spiritual reality, to expose them to it, to talk about it, to teach them the truths of the Scripture, and to involve them in church and other Christian activities and relationships.

Author/speaker Josh McDowell has many creative ideas for helping his children grow in their personal relationship with God. He says:

> I've committed myself over the last year to helping my children determine their values. Often I set up an ethical or moral situation—it's like a game for them—and ask them how they would respond. As we discuss the cor-

rect response, we go beyond what the Bible says, for behind every admonition in Scripture is an aspect of the character of God that it relates to. So instead of just taking my kids back to the Bible, I take them back to the very nature of God. Their motivation becomes a person and not a book. Isn't it better to say, "I don't do this because God is truth, or God is love"?

For example, I might set up a situation in which somebody lied. I'll say, "Why is it wrong to lie?" Because the Bible says, "Thou shalt not lie." But why does the Bible say, "Thou shalt not lie"? "Because God is truth."[1]

A Good Character

The second wish I would make for each of my children is a good character. Why is a good character important? "A good name is to be more desired than great riches, favor is better than silver and gold" (Proverbs 22:1).

Character determines so much in our lives. It influences our reputation, and our reputation affects our relationship with people, our confidence level and our ability to achieve. Our character helps to determine the contributions we will make in life. It will be instrumental in giving us peace of mind and a clear conscience.

What are the most important character qualities to develop in our children? Those qualities which influence the greatest areas of life probably are integrity, responsibility, humility, generosity, discernment, kindness, self-discipline and a sense of humor.

Character building is a lifelong process, but we can help our children start. Again, let's use our **MOST** outline.

MODEL

As always, the most important thing we can do is to model good character. Our children follow what we do more than what we say. If they see us consistently break traffic laws, they absorb that as the acceptable norm. On the other hand, if they see us tell a salesclerk she undercharged us, they will learn that being honest and truthful is important, even when it's to our disadvantage. When children see integrity, responsibility, humility, generosity, and other good character qualities demonstrated in parents' lives day by day, they assume that that's what should be true in their lives as well.

OBSERVE

We can teach our children to observe good and bad character traits in the lives of people they come in contact with. We can talk about the choices those people make and the consequences of their choices. When a friend has been bossy, we talk about how that affects us and why it's not a good quality. We talk about why Pinocchio's nose grows so long and what's wrong with lying. We point out the good qualities of Laura Ingalls in *Little House on the Prairie* as an encouragement to obedience and hard work.

We should be sure our children are exposed, through reading, media and personal interaction, to people who will demonstrate the right kind of character qualities. It's also appropriate and advisable to discuss what God says about character qualities as we see them exhibited in others.

SUPPORT

We need to support our children as they attempt to make right choices for their lives. When they are very young, we can dictate what they will do and what they won't do, protecting them from the consequences of wrong choices. As they grow older, though, they need to come to understand the impact that some activities, or certain music, or particular friends, or television, or various other kinds of entertainment might have on them and their minds and their values.

We can help them make good choices, such as bringing a bike in so it doesn't get rained on and become rusty. We can help them choose to be disciplined and to do their homework so they might have time for a fun activity.

We want to help our children learn to make "heroic

decisions." They need to learn to try new things, to dare to do something that is a little frightening, and to say no to the small temptations. Then they will be better prepared to make the hard decisions, such as taking a stand against peer pressure that could lead to using drugs, or drinking, or other detrimental activities.

TRAIN

Much of character development will occur as a way of life, but we should seek to teach our children what is right and what is wrong. We must prepare the foundation so they are equipped to make right choices in life. Our teaching should be creative. One of the best things is to make up what-if stories that allow the child to think through the consequences of a certain activity. For example, you might ask your child, "What if you hadn't done your homework one evening and your teacher asked you at school the next day why you hadn't turned your homework in—what would you say to her?"

A child might be tempted to say, "I forgot to bring it," or "I didn't feel well," or "I lost it," or make up some other excuse. It is important for him to understand the value of giving an honest and truthful response and accepting the consequences of his own lack of discipline.

It helps to make learning fun. Games such as Choices or Scruples can be used to help teach good character qualities.

Most important, we must teach our children about the person of God, about His character and what's important to Him. We need to teach them about the power that is available to them through the Holy Spirit to do what is right, to choose wisely, and to make good decisions.

A Useful Life

The third wish I have for my children is a useful life. What is a useful life? It could be defined as utilizing your gifts and abilities and talents for the glory of God and the benefit of others.

Why is it important? God has created each of us for a purpose. He has given us gifts, talents and skills, and He expects us to use them, to multiply them, and to be accountable for good stewardship of what He's given us. Therefore it's essential that we help our children discover what God has for them.

A useful life is the primary means through which God gives us our sense of value. It allows us to enjoy our lives and to feel that we are contributing something significant.

The world needs people who will contribute—society is increasingly in trouble as people become more consumers than contributors, looking more for what they can get than for what they can offer. Our children can realize that they can be a blessing when they contribute, whether it's in the home, at school or church, with their friends, or later in the workplace. As they learn to walk closely with God and to be good stewards of what He has given them, God will accomplish His purposes in and through them.

How do we help our children develop useful lives? Once again, let's use our **MOST** outline.

MODEL

As in everything else, the first thing we must do is model it. Our children must see us utilizing our skills, talents, gifts, training—all that God has given us. They must recognize our stewardship. They must see us contributing to their own lives, to the lives of others, and to society. They must see us being useful.

Even as we model it, we must explain to them what we're doing and why. Just before Steve and I left for a few days away to write, we explained to our children why we needed to be gone. Debbie responded, "I'm glad I have a mom and a dad who write." I'm glad I have a daughter who sees me endeavoring to be a good steward of what God has given me.

OBSERVE

We need to observe our children. We need to seek to understand their interests, their abilities, their "bent" in life. My children are quite different from each other. Debbie appears to be an active, aggressive leader. She has a plan and wants to make sure things happen her way.

Michelle, on the other hand, is much more relaxed. She is creative and imaginative, and makes up stories for herself and for others. If we are to help our children develop useful lives, we must discern their strengths and potential.

SUPPORT

We can support our children by providing opportunities for them to discover what they're good at, what they enjoy, and where God has gifted them. We can expose them to a variety of possibilities — sports, music, computers, art, books, theater — and support and affirm them as they experiment with different things. When they falter, we can offer encouragement to help them get up and try again or move on to something else. The atmosphere and the attitudes we offer are crucial to their feelings of confidence as they seek to discover what God wants them to be.

TRAIN

As our children discover where they want to concentrate, what their areas of gift and ability are, we must help them learn to become proficient. We must provide the training they need. That might mean continued participation in an activity or taking a special class, or joining a group, or choosing a major in college. Appropriate training will be a key for helping our children develop useful lives.

Pray and Plan

If we're really to see our wishes for our children come true, we must be committed to do our part. First we must pray, for ultimately God is the one who must build our children into the people He created them to be. We must pray for them daily, for their needs, their fears, their opportunities, their spiritual lives. We must ask God for His involvement in every area of their lives.

Then we must do our part—we must plan. Oops. Did I lose you with that? Plan for our children? Yes. If we want them to grow in a relationship with God, to develop a good character and to have a useful life, we must plan. It won't happen accidentally. Much growth will occur as we live out the things that we believe before and with our children, but we will see so much more fulfillment if we provide specific direction.

Scripture tells us we are involved in a training program: "Train up a child in the way he should go, and when he is old he will not turn from it" (Proverbs 22:6). We are usually taught that this means if we train up a child in the way God would have us—the way of Scripture and God's truth—then when he is old he will live by those principles.

This universal application is generally true. However, in *You and Your Child,* Charles Swindoll adds further enlightenment to this verse. He indicates that the Hebrew words for "the way he should go" mean to train up a child in the way that child, as an individual, is designed and created to go. In other words, we, with the child, are to discover what personality traits God has put into that child. Then we are to help the child work with those gifts—his "bent"—and choose the way God would have him go.

Planning doesn't have to be complicated or scary. Many people have made and implemented plans to help their children develop. Let me just share a few of these to give you some ideas.

Bobb Biehl, a management consultant and teacher, uses a simple, two-part plan to help his children grow and develop: (1) He teaches high values to his children; and (2) he is committed to his children. In the area of high values he stresses spiritual growth, honesty as the cornerstone of character, and teachability as the key to personal growth.

Under his own commitment, he first recognizes that the child is that child and not someone else. Second, he helps his child win. And third, he works toward achieving the best for that child. He says he has found, especially as his children have grown older, that this simple approach keeps focused on the essentials, and he does not try to cram a lot of information or instruction into his children.

Dr. Kay Kuzma, director of the Parent Scene radio ministry, offers a more systematic approach. She has chosen thirteen qualities she would like to see developed in her children: faithfulness, orderliness, self-discipline, happiness, perseverance, honesty, thoughtfulness, efficiency, responsibility, respect, enthusiasm, humility and peacefulness. She emphasizes one quality each week, repeating each of them four times a year.

For her family the major activities occur at breakfast time. Each week she picks an appropriate song that helps teach that week's quality and a Bible verse that encourages it. Then she looks for various possibilities for bringing this quality into their discussion and life each day of that week. She considers songs, Bible stories, Bible characters, great people, other stories, memory verses, what-if situations and various activities for understanding or application.[2]

This plan, of course, requires a great deal of planning and commitment. If done well, there is great likelihood these qualities will be instilled in the children's lives.

Don and Sue Myers, parents of five grown children who are all serving God, offer these five principles:

1. *Dedicated discipline.* This requires patience, persistence, consistency. It involves loving enough to set and enforce clear boundaries.

2. *Persevering prayer.* This involves praying consistently and regularly for all our children. It includes praying for major decisions they will make both now and in the future.

3. *Holy heroes.* It is important that children have heroes they can look up to with respect. The parents should help "create" these heroes by building up people who are good to emulate. The heroes of the parents should become the heroes of the children. We especially seek to make the people in God's work heroes.

4. *Making memories.* Whatever you do, do it with style. Make it memorable. Give plenty of hooks to your activities that enable the children to remember the good times.

5. *Quality cues.* Observe carefully to find out what the child considers quality time. Seek to do the things the child values more than the things the parent values.

A Way-of-Life Plan

We have a plan for each of our children that falls somewhere in the midst of these others. Our plan is somewhat detailed and written out, but the application of it is mostly informal and way-of-life. As we plan for each child, we consider two areas: (1) qualities that should be true of every child of God; and (2)character, personality traits and abilities that God seems to have put into each child's life.

We have listed a number of areas of life in which we want to see our children develop: spiritual, character, social, intellectual, creative, physical, financial understanding, and an understanding of their heritage. For each one we determine what kinds of things we would like to see happen and then name some activities that would help us move in that direction.

For example, under spiritual development we want our children to understand the importance of God in everyday life. So we talk about Him often, pray spontaneously and regularly, and relate life events and decisions to God and His character.

Under character development one of our goals is to develop responsibility. Appropriate activities include giving them regular responsibilities such as making beds, setting the table and feeding pets. These responsibilities increase as the children grow older. We also emphasize to them the value of hard work.

Under intellectual development we read to them and encourage them to read. We especially emphasize helping them learn to think by asking "why" and "how" questions. We want them to be able to think through logical results and consequences of various actions.

One of the things that we try to do under creative development is to expose the children to many different kinds of creative expression. We provide lots of materials, such as paper, blank books, art supplies, tapes and music makers, to help them feel free to express themselves creatively.

In appendix B at the end of this book you will find our plan for our children when they were three and five. This may be of help to you.

Although our use of the plan is fairly informal, we do schedule certain activities, such as attendance at a cultural event or a visit to the Children's Museum or soccer practice. We have set up a bulletin board activity center at our kitchen table. It includes Scripture verses and a world map, some of our kids' art and pictures of some of the people we pray for.

We review our plan from time to time so that we have in our minds what we're trying to teach and develop. Then when the opportunities arise, we are alert to capitalize on them.

For example, we have a family outing once a month. Before we go on that outing Steve and I both read through the plan so that we are aware of some of the things we want to teach. We want to be together as a family and to enjoy ourselves, but sometimes we also include specific purposes. If we go ice skating, we are helping our children develop physically as well as gain the experience of trying new or difficult things. If we go to the zoo, we hope to expose them to God's creation and all the variety of animals that He has made. If we go on a picnic, we enjoy the fellowship with each other, but we might also choose a subject to talk about.

We have further refined our plan in the area of discipline because this is such a difficult area. Probably the most important element in our discipline outline is the list of five guiding rules that we seek to teach our children. We have a number of specific rules, but the more we can have general rules that cover a spectrum of different kinds of activities, the more each child will learn to make her own decisions about what is right and what is wrong.

Our five rules are:

> We do not hurt God.
> We do not hurt self.
> We do not hurt others.
> We do not hurt things or animals.
> We do unto others as we would have them do unto us.

When situations come up that require correction and discipline, we seek to relate them to one of these rules. Thus the child learns to see how what she is doing might violate one of these guidelines, and so will be equipped to make a wiser choice in the future.

This chapter is by no means an exhaustive treatment of helping our children develop into significant, contributing people. It is just a beginning, a spark. Many additional sources of help and ideas are listed in appendix A.

Children are created in the image of God and by God for very specific purposes. We have an incredible responsibility and privilege to help them grow into the individuals God created them to be. We can help them establish and build a relationship with God. We can enable them to develop godly character. And we can help them discover "the way" God has for each of them, and guide them toward building useful lives.

6
Significance in Reaching Out

Think back over the past week. Who has ministered to you during that time?

Perhaps it was your husband who did a special job for you so you wouldn't have to do it. Possibly it was your child who drew a picture for you, or a neighbor who made a meal while you were sick. Perhaps it was a friend who encouraged you when you were down, or someone who told you that you did a good job. Maybe it was that person who reminded you that God loves you even when the circumstances are difficult.

These are all ministry. Remember, ministry is just being available to God to care, to love, to serve, to step into His opportunities to touch a life. We have talked at some length about ministry to our families, in particular to our children. Now let's move on to the why's and how-to's of ministering beyond our families, of being available to God to care and to touch lives outside our homes.

Ministry can be formal; it can be organized. It is appropriate that we have structures to help us minister to others — a Sunday school class, a Bible study, a counseling hot line, a church outreach program. But much of our ministry should be what we do in our day-to-day lives as we step into the opportunities God provides.

I have asked myself: Is that really necessary? I have a husband and two young children. I'm very busy. If I'm doing a good job caring for my husband and my children, I don't really have time to look beyond my family. Or do I?

Why Reach Out?

And I have answered myself: Yes, I believe I must accept another arena of ministry God has for me.

It is clear to me that every one of us who is a child of God should be available to Him. I must reach out and minister beyond my family. I see four reasons for this.

People Need Us

The first reason is that people need us. Our world is in pain. People—where we work, in our neighborhoods, at the grocery store, everywhere we go—need someone to care, someone to love them, someone to listen to them, someone to give to them. Most of all they need someone to tell them about Jesus Christ. They need to hear that message as well as see it lived in our lives.

People need us. Yes, they really need God—but God has chosen us as His channels, His ambassadors.

God Commands It

Second, God commands it. He really does! Ministry is a choice, but it is not an option. It is a command of God. Every child of God has been commissioned to tell those who don't know Him of His love and forgiveness: "But you will receive power when the Holy Spirit has come on you; and you will be My witnesses" (Acts 1:8). "This is to my Father's glory, that you bear much fruit, showing yourselves to be my disciples . . . you did not choose me, but I chose you to go and bear fruit—fruit that will last" (John 15:8,16).

We also are to reach out to our brothers and sisters in Christ. Even as we grow to maturity in Christ, God's Word tells us that we are to play a role in that same process for other believers: "And the things you have heard me say in the presence of many witnesses entrust to reliable men who will also be qualified to teach others" (2 Timothy 2:2).

God's Word also tells us to serve one another in love (Galatians 5:13), to bear one another's burdens (Galatians 6:2), to provide for those in need (1 John 3:17), to demonstrate love with our actions and not just with our words (1 John 3:18), to comfort those who hurt (2 Corinthians 1:3-7), and to show hospitality (Romans 12:13). God commands that we be involved in ministry.

We Need It

The third reason? *We* need it. People need it, and God commands it—but we need it, too. If our entire lives focus only on our own family and close friends, on our own needs and interests, we are the losers. A job can be so all-consuming that we neglect our friends, our families, ourselves. Equally, we can become so absorbed in family that we forget the world Christ died for. We can lose our perspective on life, our vision of a world full of people going to a Christless eternity if someone doesn't tell them about Jesus.

We are refreshed when we venture outside our own lives and problems and become involved in the lives of others. It is important for our spiritual health that we give out what God is building into our lives, and it is important for our emotional health that we not be overly self-centered. We also need to be challenged. It's so easy to be comfortable when most of the people with whom we live and work and share are those who think the way we do and agree with us.

Our Children Need It

The fourth reason for ministering beyond our families is that our children need it. They need to see us reaching out to others. How else are they going to know that that's what the Christian life is about? They need to know that it is more than going to church once or twice a week, saying grace and bedtime prayers, and reading the Bible, as important as those things are. Our children must understand that the Christian life is walking closely with God in the power of His Spirit. It is being available to be and do all that God has for us. It is stepping into those God-given opportunities to touch lives.

Here is what some mothers have to say about the importance of ministry beyond their families.

> Susie: I feel that a full-time mother and housewife needs her own spiritual development and feelings of self-worth (after facing the same recurring pile of dirty laundry) that can come from reaching outside her home for Christ, no matter how small an effort.

> Judy: I have a responsibility to the Great Commission to reach non-Christians and to disciple those who receive Christ as well as other Christians. I believe the exercising of my spiritual gifts will involve me in ministry in others' lives as an example to my children, and will help form in them a heart of compassion for the needs of others. Also my life is kept in better perspective and less egocentric when I am involved with others.

> Carol: There are so many needs both within and without the body of Christ. I believe as disciples of His we're called and empowered to meet these needs. God gives us specific gifts to minister so that it will not be a burden but something we enjoy. Giving keeps us growing. It is a living demonstration to our children of a servant lifestyle. It teaches them that there is a cost to serving Christ, but also that it is worth the cost.

> Myra: I feel it's valuable, especially for my own family, for me to demonstrate what I believe is important enough to do something about, to make the sacrifices it takes to be involved.

The Greatest Example

Who provides the greatest model of ministry for us? Certainly it would be the Lord Jesus.

As we look at Him, particularly in the book of Mark, we

see Him actively involved in ministry. Throughout this account of Christ's life, Mark emphasizes Jesus' priority of caring for the spiritual needs of people, of teaching them the truths of the kingdom of God. Yet, even as He taught and spoke and forgave sins, He also met other needs day by day. He healed; He prayed for people; He cast out demons; He fed the 5,000; He welcomed the children; He served people where they had needs (Mark 1:21-27; 32-35; 38-39; 2:2-12; 4:1-2; 6:42; 9:37).

In the thirteenth chapter of John we see Jesus as the ultimate servant, demonstrating selfless caring for others as He chose to wrap a towel about Himself and wash His disciples' feet. After performing this undesirable task, He told them He was the master and yet He had served them. In the same way they were to serve others.

Jesus, in His life and in His teaching, reminds us over and over that we are to be caring, outreaching people.

One Family's Story

Art and Nancy DeMoss and their seven children have had a remarkable ministry through the years. One significant family outreach of theirs has been their evangelistic dinner parties, where literally thousands have been introduced to the Savior.

Art and son David are now home with the Lord, but the family continues to reach out to others in caring, in counseling, and most of all in evangelism. God has given them wonderful fruit as they have shared Christ abundantly.

Most of the children are now grown and all of them are involved in ministry in some way. Nancy Leigh speaks and writes about the family and revival. Mark serves as administrative assistant to the Reverend Jerry Falwell. All come home whenever possible to be a part of the family's dinner parties.

When asked, "What has caused you to have such a heart for God, such a desire to serve Him, to want to lead others

to Christ?" each one gave the same answer: "I am involved
in ministry because I saw it demonstrated in our family's
life day after day. Lives were being changed. We were available to people. We wanted to serve God and touch lives for
Him."

Because the children saw it in their family, it became
their commitment as well.

But how? How do you become a caring, outreaching person? How can you find the time? What if you feel you have
no special abilities to offer? How do you step into those opportunities that God provides?

In the next chapters we're going to look at some specific
ways you can be involved in ministry beyond your family:
on your knees, in your home, through your church, in your
community, to those in need, with your husband and
children, and to the world, as a way of life.

You will meet many women. Some are involved in informal, everyday ministries. Others have developed larger
or more structured outreaches. Whether large or small, formal or way-of-life, each ministry began with an attitude of
availability, a willingness to reach out, to care, to serve. And
each woman has, in faith, stepped into her God-given opportunity. Perhaps through their stories God will reveal an
open door—an opportunity for ministry—just for you.

7
On Your Knees

There is one ministry without which there is no power in any other. There is one ministry that must come before all others. There is one ministry that can be done anytime, anywhere, by anyone. That is the ministry of prayer.

Marilyn Wishart's prayer ministry began while she was on her knees after the birth of her third child later in life. Merran, Marilyn's daughter, almost died because of an RH problem. A total transfusion saved her life, but she was a fretful baby with an immature nervous system.

"When she was born," Marilyn says, "I came to believe the Lord wanted me back in the home. I had taught for most of my married life, and it had been hard on the other children to have both parents working.

"I felt that God had given Merran to us in a special way since He had saved her life. But being home was an adjustment. I was used to working. I was used to involvement in Sunday school, with the youth ministry and in visits to a convalescent home. All those opportunities were shut down because Merran was such a fretful baby."

Learning to Pray

"My attitude was not good," Marilyn continues. "I said, 'Lord, I want to serve You. You haven't opened any doors, so I'm just going to have to pray.' That's when I began."

When Marilyn began to try to pray while the baby slept or while she nursed her, she discovered that she didn't really know how. So her prayer became, "God, You have things You want me to pray for. Teach me how to pray."

"God would bring things to my mind and I would pray," she says. "He began to enlarge me. That whole year was the best year we've ever had. My husband's job was blessed, the children discovered new talents, they grew closer to the Lord, the baby came through well and I grew to a faith level and a knowledge of God that I had never had before. I believe God was showing me that if we do the things that He wants us to do, He will take care of our needs."

One heavy concern that God put on Marilyn's heart during that time was the needs of the Vietnamese boat people. As she saw them on TV and read about them, her heart was burdened for them. So she prayed. But she didn't know if there were any results.

A Tug on Her Heart

One day she found herself praying, "Lord, is there an island, a shelter, for these people?" So she prayed for an is-land. At the end of that prayer time, she wasn't sure she could tell anybody about it—it seemed such an impossible request. But two months later a friend gave her a pamphlet, and she read that the president of the Philippines had given an island for the boat people. "I knew then," Marilyn says, "that I had entered into an adventure in prayer that I had never comprehended before."

That kind of experience has been an important area of prayer for Marilyn—to feel the tug of the heart as God gives her things to pray for.

While Marilyn nursed her baby, she would pray for her, asking God for wisdom as to what to pray. "At first I would pray for her and for her needs. Then I began to speak of the goodness and love of God to her. I told her that God loved her, that He had a special purpose for her. I encourage any nursing mother to use that time to pray for her children. What a beautiful time to pick up the prayer watch."

After that first year Marilyn began to pray with a partner as well. Then she began meeting with a group of women in her Vancouver, British Columbia, neighborhood and they found that whenever they got together, they didn't talk — they prayed. So they began a monthly prayer meeting from 10 to 12 at night in the home of one of the women. As other women saw what God was doing in their lives and through their lives, they wanted to know how to pray as well. "Teach us," they said.

"That was a real challenge and the first step of teaching was a little scary," Marilyn says. "We put together a one-day seminar."

Marilyn's teaching on prayer began with the need to hear God's call to prayer and to respond to it. "I teach people how to hear the voice of God and to sit in His presence and to pray for other people's needs.

"I'm very practical," Marilyn adds. "I saw the need for prayer, so I began to pray for people to pray. I realized they needed to know how, so I began to pray for someone to teach them. Then I discovered I was the one to do that.

"But my real love is still praying."

The other members of Marilyn's family have become pray-ers as well. "We pray about everything. Whatever one of us is doing, the rest of us have a part because we pray. So for each of us, any ministry is the whole family's ministry.

"I believe that God wants everyone to be a prayer warrior," Marilyn emphasizes. "All a person has to do is ask the Lord, 'Where I am just now, how would You have me to pray?'

"For young mothers it's very simple. They can pray as they do their housework, or as they feed their children or watch them playing. When they think of their husbands, they can send up a prayer.

"Prayer is not complicated. It is just a relationship with the Lord Jesus Christ. God takes us on an adventure. He brings answers to prayer to encourage us, to show us that we're in the total will of God."

An Unexpected Beginning

While Linda Davis and her husband, Ev, were missionaries in Ghana, Africa, they were a part of a ministry of evangelism and discipleship—a "multiplication that grew from prayer." Believers were praying for neighbors and for evangelism in a thousand daily home prayer cells when they arrived. When they left five years later, there were about twenty-five hundred groups meeting daily.

Returning home to Chicago for Ev to attend seminary, they were dismayed to find among Christians in America so little emphasis on evangelism, and so little prayer—but so much disintegration of the Christian home and family.

As Linda looked for a ministry in Chicago, she heard of an outreach to women of influence in New York City and decided, with another young woman, to try to reach influencial women in her area. They began to call women in media, in government and in other high positions.

"But we really needed prayer for this and there were just the two of us," Linda said. "So I looked for some kind of organized prayer movement. I couldn't find even one." About that time Evelyn Christenson held a prayer seminar in the area and Linda went to that in hopes of finding other women who wanted to pray. She came away with a list of 250 women for her to organize into a prayer movement. That was the unexpected beginning of what has grown into a multi-faceted ministry of prayer for Linda.

"The first thing we did was put together a booklet called 'Prayer for Those Who Influence Your Family.' We gave this to the women so they would have a scriptural basis for beginning to pray for their families—then moving in concentric circles out toward the church, the neighborhood, the community, the government, the nation and the world."

A desire to make this a church-based prayer ministry led to a weekend prayer seminar for churches and an organized telephone prayer chain. Eventually came an opportunity to produce a daily two-minute radio broadcast on prayer for the Moody Broadcast Network. "Drawing Closer" became a joint project for Ev and Linda. At first they wrote the scripts together, but soon Linda was doing most of the writing, and Ev was taping the daily segments for the broadcast.

When Ev finished seminary, and they moved to Crestline, California, the family emphasis on prayer became a full-time ministry for him. He became the U.S. director for the Great Commission Prayer Crusade. Continuing their team ministry, Ev and Linda have been involved in revising the "Dynamics of Prayer Workshop" into a new workshop called "In His Presence."

Impact on the Family

All this emphasis on a ministry of prayer has had an impact on Linda's personal prayer life. She says, "It has not been easy for me to pray for people I don't know. That's why using the 'Prayer for Those Who Influence Your Family' booklet has been helpful. I found that I didn't always concentrate well in prayer, I started keeping a prayer journal. I wrote down everything I prayed for. This enabled me to concentrate, and it gave me a record of my prayers and of the faithfulness of God in answering them, sometimes over many years."

Prayer has had an impact on the Davis children also. "When I was doing the prayer chain in Chicago," Linda relates, "I was the one who took the requests and started the chain by calling others to pray. This was time consuming, but I could do it at home. Invariably, though, the children wanted attention at that time. I had to find ways to keep them occupied so I could make the calls—but at the same time they learned the importance of prayer. It became a part of their lives. It also has shown them that we care about being involved with them in something important. We pray with them about their teachers, their studies, their activities."

Ev and Linda's three girls, now ten, twelve and seventeen, "truly sense the importance of our ministry in prayer. It's not beyond them; they feel they are a part of it."

Maintaining Continuity

When Dean and Jan Beal went to Puerto Rico as missionaries, their daughter, Susan, was only three. Going overseas meant separation from family and from the people who had been a part of her life. In order to maintain some continuity with family and friends back home, Jan started a scrapbook of pictures and prayer for Susan. It evolved into a prayer ministry for the family together.

"At first I gathered family pictures because we wanted her to feel a part of her family and to know her roots," Jan explains. "Then we included the staff members that we worked with in Latin America. We added pictures of our leaders, and then later pictures of political leaders and current events, supporters, friends, neighbors and people to whom we were ministering.

"Each day we would open the prayer book to the next page and ask 'Who on this page do you want to pray for today?' So Susan would choose one from that page and we would pray. When we received letters from someone, we stuck them in on the appropriate page and read those before we prayed.

"We used that book for about three years, and I believe that it helped Susan to develop a spontaneity in her prayer life. Even today she'll read the newspaper or catch a news item, and her natural response is to pray for the situation."

Many other mothers have found prayer to be their most effective ministry.

Darla: When Paul was newborn, I would collect prayer requests from my husband and from friends who were serving Christ and try to pray spontaneously during the day. Now that Paul is at an age of understanding, I have him join me to pray for different needs. It helps us to feel we are affecting the world for Christ, even when we are housebound.

Fran: I keep my prayer list at the kitchen sink and pray for people all the time. I pray with the children whenever anything happens that we need to stop and pray about.

Kathy: The five of us in a carpool together were all Christians, so we began to meet once a week to pray for our children. It was an exciting ministry as we sought, not to tell about the problems of our children, but just to pray for them and to be a part of each others' lives.

Pamela: When my children were young, I began to write out my prayers because invariably one of the children would come and say, "May I have a drink of water?" I could get them a drink of water and then I could go back. I could pick up my train of thought and keep going.

Shirley: At one time God seemed to take all of my ministry opportunities away. I kept looking for some and they just weren't there. So I began to understand that He wanted me to pray. I prayed for ministry and I prayed for others, but most of all I prayed for my children. And I found increasingly that I didn't have to tell them what to do. I could just pray and God would cause them to do it.

What can you do? I'm convinced that God has for you a ministry on your knees.

In your home: Pray when you have concentrated time. Pray on the spur of the moment. Send SOS prayers. Pray for your family, your neighborhood, your church, your state, your nation, the world.

On the phone: Have a prayer partner. Be part of a telephone prayer chain. Call people when you hear of a need and pray for them. Pray about needs as you talk with friends.

With a partner: Meet regularly with a friend to pray for each other and for others. Have an informal arrangement where you know you can call on your partner to pray for you whenever you have a need, and she can call on you when she has a need.

On a prayer chain: Make yourself available to be on a phone chain within your city or church. All you will need to do is pray for the particular person or need and then call another person to pass on the request.

In your church: Be a part of a regular prayer group. Attend prayer meetings. Pray for missionaries from your church, for your pastor, for your church programs.

Through the newspaper: Pray for concerns as you read about them. Pray for those who suffer tragedies. Pray for moral and political issues that concern you. Pray for people who influence you and your life—in the media, in government, in education, in entertainment.

Through personal intercession: Maintain a specific prayer list and pray regularly for people, situations, needs and concerns.

Through the centuries men and women of God have emphasized that prayer is the most essential and effective ministry there is for reaching the lost for Christ, for building the Body of Christ, for effecting change in our world. Many have said that if they could change one thing in their lives, it would be to pray more. For many mothers prayer is the only consistent ministry to others that they can have. How special that God has given to us the most important ministry of all.

8
In Your Home

Ready for a pop quiz? Take a minute to indicate if the following statements are true or false for you.

___ 1. I like to talk on the phone.

___ 2. People feel comfortable in our home.

___ 3. I know my regular babysitter(s) well enough to know some needs she has.

___ 4. Neighborhood children frequently spend time in our home.

___ 5. I feel comfortable with people in our home.

___ 6. I enjoy writing letters.

___ 7. I am a good listener.

___ 8. I know some of my neighbors well enough to drop by to chat or ask them over for coffee.

___ 9. I read a newspaper.

___ 10. I like to pray.

If you answered *true* to any of the above questions, you could have an effective ministry in your own home. The home should be the most natural place for ministry and for demonstrating and modeling the Christian life to our families and those around us.

A Better Product

When Jerri Younkman answers the phone at her San Bernardino, California, home and discovers she has a salesperson on the line, she reaches immediately for a little card above her telephone. She smiles and reads:

"I'm sorry I cannot buy your product but, John, when someone calls to share a product with me, I like to take the opportunity to share my faith with them. I am so excited about being a Christian that I wonder if I could share briefly with you some information about how you can become a Christian."

When someone responds positively, Jerri shares the message of Christ.

"I got this idea from a friend," Jerri says. "Since then I have done it regularly, and it has helped to rejuvenate my desire to share Christ with people. It's so easy. I find I get to chat with 60 to 70 percent of the people who call. I've had very few people give me any kind of angry or resentful response. Most are positive.

"Often it's obvious that a person is busy, so sometimes I ask for a name and address and offer to send some material that would be helpful for them in coming to know God. Some have received Christ, and I've had the opportunity to follow them up. I've talked to new Christians and have done some follow-up in their lives. Once I had a Christian woman call back after she finished work to say how excited she was at what I was doing. I've also talked with those who have not been interested, but they've almost always been polite.

"So you see, even if all your kids are sick or you yourself are sick, this is a way you can still reach out and share Christ. Anyone can do it."

"What Could I Do?"

When Barbara Jakob's first child was born, she took her along as she continued teaching seminars and training courses for evangelism. But when her second child was born a little later, that was no longer possible. "Being a very active person, though, I just couldn't sit at home and see all these people who needed Christ. What could I do?"

As Barbara got to know other mothers of young children in her Zurich, Switzerland, neighborhood, she observed that most of them were frustrated and had almost no one with whom to interact and talk. And they desperately wanted help in raising their children.

So Barbara began to visit places where young mothers might be—the park, the child health center, even on the street. She would introduce herself to a mother, almost always startling the lady, and then Barbara would invite her over for coffee, so they could talk and get to know each other. Most of the mothers were eager to make a new friend.

Then Barbara would say, "We have a Christian women's group and we're talking about a book that tells about raising children. Would you be interested in coming?"

In three or four weeks she had gathered together a group of twelve women. A friend began to use the same approach, and soon they had more than twenty women. They split into two groups. Talks on child rearing often led into spiritual needs, and eventually some of the women received Christ. A Bible study was started.

"We provide a babysitter at the home so women can bring their children. There is very little child care available for European women, and this is one of the few opportunities they have to go somewhere. The idea has been so popular that now many other Christians are leading groups and there are about thirty in the Zurich area and maybe fifty more throughout Switzerland.

"Leading the group is easy," Barbara says, "because we provide the material for discussion. The leader does not have to be an expert herself.

"One of the best things about this is that I'm not out much," Barbara says. "We have one evening committee meeting a month, and I have the Bible study series for five weeks, one evening a week.

"My children are very excited about this ministry. I can be a good mother, and the more I give of myself to other people, the more my family profits."

A Warm Atmosphere

Two dozen people crowded into Kathy Wille's living room. They had just finished eating some Texas barbecue and were now settling down to listen to a speaker talk about "Maximizing Your Potential: A Biblical Perspective on Managing Yourself." An hour later the audience had received some practical ideas on planning for their lives, scheduling their time and following their schedules—and seven of them indicated that they had invited Jesus Christ into their lives. They would be followed up and discipled by those who had brought them to this dinner.

Only about half of those attending had known each other—they were from the same Sunday school class. Each of them had invited a few friends or neighbors who they thought might not be Christians but who might be interested in learning how to maximize themselves and in how to know Christ in a personal way.

Invitations were made up; people were invited, and then called again with an offer to pick them up. Kathy assigned different class members to bring parts of the meal and decorated her home to make people feel welcome.

When they arrived, they played a low-key get-acquainted game and had some lemonade and hors d'oeuvres. Several tables had been set up for dinner, which was enjoyed in a relaxed way. The message that was given fulfilled its promise of helpful ideas for the people on managing themselves. The message of Christ was included as a tasteful and integral part of the presentation.

This was the second such dinner that Kathy and her husband, Jim, had had. Why did they do it?

"We do this because it is so much fun and such an easy way to share with our friends and neighbors about Christ. We invite them to our home where they can feel comfortable. We offer them some content from a qualified person on a subject that would interest them. And as a part of that we show them how Christ is related to every area of life. Our children are happy playing with some neighbors or with their grandparents, and we are able to use our home to help people come into the kingdom."

Using Homes for Ministry

Other women also have discovered effective ways to use their homes for ministry.

Carol: We have had three foster children living in our home for four to eight months. We would do that again. We also have had alcoholics and drug addicts live with us for a period of time. We do that on a month-to-month basis, and we evaluate the effectiveness at the end of each month and decide whether we should continue.

Susie: Neighbors provide ministry. Even a seemingly quiet, normal neighborhood is filled with old age, loneliness, cancer, death and suffering, and divorce with its effects on children. It is abounding with non-Christians and cultural Christians.

Linda: When my younger boy was five I had a small, unofficial preschool in our home. There were seven boys around our table in the living room two days a week.

Donna Lynn: Letter writing is a fabulous ministry that few people take the time for. The children are able to do this as well. They write letters and draw pictures for many people—those in the hospital who are discouraged or lonely, and others we want to befriend.

Carolyn: I invite neighborhood children to play with my children and then ask their moms to come for lunch or coffee when it's time to pick the children up.

Kathy: Recently I had a very effective "follow-up" session on the phone with a relatively new believer. Neither of us could get out of our homes, so I spent about twenty-five minutes with her on the phone going over Scripture and answering her questions.

Judy: When my husband has traveled, I have tried to invite some woman who is alone with her children over for lunch or dinner or a picnic. Our children are encouraged to be hosts and to extend hospitality to these children. Sometimes Bible study is included in these get-togethers, but often it is just for companionship.

Sandi: Many international students are very lonely, so we have often tried to have them into our home to befriend them, to help meet their needs, and then hopefully to be able to share Christ with them as well.

More Ideas

The ideas for ministering in and from your home are almost endless.

Using the telephone: Call someone to share prayer requests or just to talk. Call absent Sunday school members to tell them they were missed. Call the sick. Be available to those who call you. Share Christ with those who call. Work on a pregnancy counseling hot line or some other crisis hot line. Call to invite people to church. Call appropriate people about moral or political issues. Make phone calls for a political candidate.

Hospitality at home: Invite people over to visit. Have a potluck in the neighborhood and help people make new friends. Invite new people at church to come over for a meal after services. Have a Bible study or prayer group in your home. Open your home to out-of-town guests, to international students or visitors, to visiting missionaries, or to unwed mothers. Babysit for others in your home. Invite your neighbors over for coffee or for dinner or for a backyard barbecue. Get ideas from *Cooking from the Heart—A Guide to Evangelistic Entertaining* (Here's Life Publishers, revised 1988).

Neighborhood children: Share Christ with them. Invite them to Sunday school or church. Invite them to spend the night. Invite their parents to church. Read Bible stories to the children. Provide love and security. Have a Good News or backyard club for children.

Babysitters: Share Christ with your sitter. Help meet her needs. Help meet her family's needs. Invite the sitter and her family to church.

Writing letters: Send cards or notes for special occasions. Write letters to children. Write letters of encouragement. Find a pen pal. Write to your congressmen, TV sponsors, local TV stations and newspapers about moral and political issues. Write to church leaders to encourage them. Write to missionaries.

Neighbors: Seek to meet their needs. Go out of your way to get to know them. Express love and encouragement. Include them in some of your activities. Share Christ.

Listening: Let people talk about their problems. Listen to your children. Listen to your husband. Ask questions so people will share.

Read newspapers: Pray about issues or incidents. Write letters to the editor. Send help to the needy. Write to people in the news and share Christ with them. Send church information to new parents.

If home is the most significant place in the world, it certainly should be one of the best places for ministry. Home should be a place in which and from which we love, we care, we serve, we reach out, and we look for God-given opportunities to step in and touch lives for Him.

9
Through Your Church

About fifty women gathered in the church fellowship hall one Tuesday morning. They chatted amiably over their coffee and cookies and then took their seats for a twenty-minute Bible study on the attributes of God.

This week the study was on God's righteousness. Every Christian there got a bigger perspective of how holy God is. Any who might not have known Christ began to grasp God's righteousness, their own sin and their need of a Savior.

After the Bible study the women separated into their chosen classes. Some went to a tape study on the philosophy of Christian womanhood, others to a writing class. A third class was on candlewicking. That evening the sessions would be repeated for those who weren't able to attend the morning groups. The next eight-week session included a Bible study on understanding God's wonderful love and plan for us, with classes on mothering, cooking, prayer and calligraphy. During each session church members were able to grow in their fellowship with each other. But more important, they were able to bring friends from the community into the church to participate in practical and helpful learning as well as to hear about Jesus Christ and how He might affect their lives. During each session one or two people indicated that they had invited Christ into their lives.

In our church this was called "Women for Creative Living." In other churches it has other names: "Women's Ministries," or "Reaching Out, Reaching In," or "Mary and Martha Ministries." Always it seeks to minister to the women in the church through teaching and fellowship. And often it seeks to reach out into the community by drawing those who have not yet met Christ into a relationship with His children.

One of the greatest opportunities for ministry for mothers is through their churches. We go to church — we're going to be there anyway. Care for our children is usually available. And the many programs provide a wide variety of ministry opportunities for us.

A Caring, Loving Place

Kathie Stranger of Yucaipa, California, continually has looked for opportunities to serve in her church. She first began working as a volunteer in children's church with the four- and five-year-olds. "I had always done a lot of babysitting and I really loved children. The church school needed some help, so I made myself available.

"When my first daughter, Gretchen, was born and started to go to the baby nursery, I realized there were needs in that program," Kathie explains. "I was not satisfied with the facility or with the degree of developmental motivation shown in my daughter's care and thought there must be ways to make it a more interesting and communicative place.

"I had been working full time and now was home with a baby who was very good and slept most of the time. I had almost nothing to do, so I volunteered to work on the baby nursery. At that time we were building a new Christian Education building for our church, so we were able to begin with the actual design and layout of the room that we would use. We wanted it to be attractive, comfortable and efficient. We wanted the babies to enjoy being there, and we wanted the mothers and fathers to feel good about leaving their children there."

Kathie sought to take the capable staff members who were there and help them organize for greater effectiveness both in the use of their skills and in the care that they provided for the children.

Kathie was also greatly concerned that "people see our whole early childhood area as not just babysitting. In the nursery we wanted the children to learn of God's love and care for them through the loving care they experienced."

In the years that followed she began to work on developing a program for the 4's and 5's that would help them learn about the Christian life and grow in it. Then she worked on programs for the 3's and then the toddlers. By this time her second child was in preschool three mornings a week. Her children had often gone to church with her as she worked in the nursery and the other children's rooms. They had been the objects of testing curriculum that she developed for each age level.

But now the time seemed right for Kathie to formalize her activities with the church and she took a part-time job as early childhood director, spending at least twenty hours a week working to develop, structure and maintain what she had been building with the help of the other staff in the children's program.

"God gave me a vision for the kind of program that would truly minister to our children and our parents. And I was willing to put in a lot of hard work and energy. I felt defeated many, many times, but God always brought the special people who would labor with me just to give me the courage to continue."

Kathie passed on her responsibilities to others when she had twins a couple of years ago. Now, as the babies are getting a little older, she is looking for other places in the church where God would have her minister again.

Opportunities for a Single Mom

Merri Hawkins is a single mom in Redlands, California. She is a full-time student, and she works half time, five days a week. She cares for her three-year-old son, Kristopfer. And she has a ministry to junior high girls.

Merri experiences all of the pressures that go with being a working, studying, single mother. She has to arrange care for her son; she has to be concerned about her income; she has to find time to study; she has to care for her child when he's sick.

She's in a good situation, though. She lives at home with her family, so she does not have to handle her life all by herself and she has a source of financial help. She also receives some support from her son's father.

On the two mornings a week that Merri goes to school, her son goes to a preschool facility. On Mondays, Wednesdays and Fridays she is able to be at home with him, and during some of that time she studies while he plays or watches TV. And she studies after he goes to bed at night. She works from 2:30 to 6:30 every afternoon, and her mother and brother help care for Kristopfer while she works.

Still, the pressures are there. Merri considers her ministry in her church one of the main resources to help her cope with the stress she experiences.

When Merri first returned to the Lord and started getting active in her church, she wasn't sure where she would fit in. Being a single parent, she didn't feel comfortable with the college students. She enjoyed the singles ministry, but was younger than most of the people involved there.

Then several Sundays in a row her church made an appeal for workers. "I felt I wasn't growing, and I decided this was something I could do. I thought I'd work with fifth or sixth grade, but I ended up with junior high and I like it.

"On Sunday mornings I teach a group of about five seventh-grade girls. We are using a wonderful curriculum called 'Building Christian Character.' It goes through qualities like patience, perseverance, faith, love and the fruit of the Spirit."

Merri puts a lot of effort into keeping her girls involved. She calls them and sends them cards. "And now we're getting ready to start working on an outreach to draw other seventh-grade girls into our class."

Merri's small group of girls is part of a broader junior high program that includes not only the Sunday morning study time but also a Saturday evening activity called Son City. "They play games and have refreshments and Bible study. I try to go every other week. There are usually about sixty junior and senior high kids. It's fun and it helps the kids to bring in their friends who are not exposed to the gospel."

Merri is expected to be in church not only on Sunday mornings, but also on Sunday evenings, as an example to the young people. In addition, every Wednesday evening she attends a training session to review the previous week's lesson and to prepare for the coming week. "We try to make the material apply to what's going on in the kids' lives.

"This has helped me to grow so much in finding out who I am in the Lord and the direction He has for my life," Merri says. "I think my ministry is the learning part of my life. I wouldn't have grown with the Lord as much as I have if I hadn't had this ministry. Kristopfer is a very important part of my life, but he is not my whole life. I think the Lord has other things for me to do as well as being a mom."

Mothers of Preschoolers

Marilyn Barnes had been accustomed to an active ministry before her first child, Kristy, was born. So Marilyn began the process of looking for opportunities to minister while she was at home with her daughter. She has two more children now, and God has given her a multi-faceted ministry that includes fellowship, outreach to her Denver, Colorado, community, ministry to her children, and a group of women to disciple.

Her ministry is through MOPS—Mothers Of Pre-Schoolers. MOPS began in Colorado in the early 1970s when a few mothers decided they wanted to have an outreach ministry to other mothers. Now there are hundreds of MOPS groups throughout the country, all guided by the parent organization in Denver—MOPS, Inc.—which is staffed entirely by volunteers. (See appendix A.)

A MOPS group can start when approval from MOPS, Inc., is given to a church to use the name for its ministry to mothers. One requirement is that the church statement of faith agree with the MOPS statement of faith.

The 9 to 11:30 A.M. time begins with fellowship and refreshments, followed by sharing, caring and preparing segments. In the sharing segment a speaker shares on some topic of interest to mothers of preschoolers. One time the subject might be a practical area such as hospitality. Another time it could be a spiritual area such as "deepening your relationship with God." Often a mother shares her own experiences in raising small children and how the Lord has helped her.

Then the women break into small groups of about ten for the caring time. Leaders guide the discussion as the women talk about practical applications of what the speaker said, or they share needs. They seek to encourage and help each other to cope with various problems in their lives, especially related to rearing children. The preparing time is for crafts. Each woman has a chance to start and finish some small project that demonstrates her creativity and provides a sense of accomplishment.

"MOPS has been such a great opportunity for me," says Marilyn. "We are able to help the women learn more about the Lord and about themselves, to have fellowship with each other, to exchange ideas and information and to have a sense of satisfaction and fulfillment in doing something with their hands.

"Because I had had some experience in evangelism and discipleship, I was given the responsibility of leading and training the leaders of our small groups. I helped them to prepare testimonies of how they had come to know Christ, and each of them will be sharing her testimony in her care group during the year.

"I meet with the group leaders once a month to go over what we'll be doing in the next month," Marilyn explains. "Throughout the year they will share various aspects of the Christian life, such as how to know Christ, how to be filled with the Spirit and how to share Christ with others."

Probably 25 to 30 percent of the MOPS participants are not members of Marilyn's church. Many of them have come to know Christ and joined the church as a result of participating in MOPS. In fact, two of Marilyn's group leaders met the Lord through the program, then joined the church and now are leading others. The group has grown from an original thirty to more than 130 in four years.

"This has been such a blessing for me," Marilyn relates. "Where else can a mother find a group of committed women to disciple? And then see them multiply their lives into others' lives? At the same time my children thoroughly enjoy the Moppets program. Stories, music, playtime, snacktime and crafts all keep the children entertained and help them to learn about Christ as well."

Singles Outreach

Elisa Bloomsburg is probably the youngest member of her church singles group. Four years old, she goes to most of the social activities with her mom, Ruth, who heads the outreach program of the singles ministry.

Ruth became a Christian as a young child but drifted away from the Lord. When Elisa was born she returned to

the Lord, and soon after moving to Redlands, California,
she became involved at a church with an active singles
program.

"There is a closeness in the singles group," Ruth says.
"The director really ministers to us and that was something
I needed. Before I realized it, I was moving into a leadership position. I had attended various activities and noticed
that none of the people on the singles council had children.
I felt they didn't have the whole picture of the needs of
singles, so I became involved."

As outreach chairman, Ruth's job is to help the singles
group contact people in the community, minister to them
and draw them into the group. "We tended to wait for somebody to come to us, but now we're seeking them. We
sponsor a lot of social activities, like a picnic in the park or
a game time before a churchwide revival service. We play
volleyball and other games. We encourage our members to
invite their friends and then, hopefully, they will feel comfortable attending church or a special service in the future."

Ruth's church activities include Afterglows each Sunday evening at a different person's house, Sunday morning
services, the singles Sunday school class, a monthly single
adult leadership training meeting and a monthly planning
meeting. There is a Bible study on Tuesday nights, but
Ruth finds that she is not able to attend that.

"The singles group has been good for Elisa because it is
like an extended family, especially since we're not with our
family," Ruth says. "They give her a lot of attention. She
is often the only young child there, so she gets to sit on
everyone's lap. It's been good for the singles as well."

Because the singles ministry has been such an important part of Ruth and Elisa's life and spiritual growth, when
she recently moved to Washington state she immediately
looked for a church in which to get involved. In California
Ruth was working full time and Elisa was in preschool. Now
she lives with her sister and her husband and their two

young children. She and her sister trade off working a half day each running a sports store the family owns. They take turns caring for the children on the other half of the day.

"This is a real answer to prayer," Ruth says. "It's not the way I would have expected God to answer, but it fits all the needs we have.

"And whatever church we get involved in I hope to start a young women's discipleship program. I think reaching out to others helps the person who reaches out as much as it helps the others. At least that's what I have experienced.

"Being a single mom is a hard job. I think my mothering experience is enhanced by Christian service. I think it is important for my child to see that in my life — to see that I serve Christ."

Ministry in a Church

Many women have found the church a natural place for ministry.

Coryne: I taught a women's Bible study one morning a week and discipled a new Christian in my home during my baby's nap time. I tried to speak at evangelistic coffees, but didn't like that so I trained some others to do it. That became the main outreach in our church women's group. Some women spoke, some had coffees in their home, and others cared for the children in the nursery.

Patti: When my older son was in the fifth and sixth grades, we became aware that not much was being done with children in our church. So we began what we called "Great Escapes" with the fifth and sixth graders. Once a month we took them on some kind of event. Next month we will be taking them to an orphanage to meet the children there and spend some time with them. Another time the children visited an abused children's center and took gifts to the children. We had made a number of the gifts ourselves.

There are usually about twenty kids, and many of them don't know the Lord. We plan to bring in a speaker

soon who will talk about rock music. Over a period of time
we have opportunities to share Christ with these kids.

Wanda: When we moved to a new church, my husband
was going to school and working full time, and we had
one young daughter. I began to attend a small women's
Bible study in our church for which babysitting was
provided. There I found non-Christians and young, immature Christians, all with one thing in common—they
were struggling with young children. Before long I was
leading the study, which helped to provide spiritual
resources for them.

When my husband finished school, he became active
in the church and we spent two years leading a growth
group. It was exciting to give these people their first taste
of discipleship.

Donna: I have always felt that it was important to be
"where my children are" and so have worked in their
areas of the church. I helped to start a Pioneer Girl's
work in our church and worked as a leader for about five
years. For many years I worked with the vacation Bible
school, serving as the director one year. As my children
have grown, I have branched into other areas of serving
in the church.

In case you haven't yet seen, through these stories, a
ministry you might have in your church, let me suggest just
a few more areas that perhaps will spark an idea for you!

Children: Teach or assist in a Sunday school class,
children's church, boys' and girls' week-day programs, day
care or mother's day out programs, vacation Bible school.

Adults: Teach or serve as an officer in a Sunday school
class. Write a newsletter for your Sunday school class. Call
people for your class. Teach a Bible study. Get onto a prayer
chain. Work with the singles program. Welcome new
people. Counsel those who are hurting.

Outreach: Invite people to church and to Sunday
school class. Start an aerobics class. Participate in visita-
tion. Take an evangelism class. Speak up concerning moral
concerns in your community.

The mission field: Go on the mission field, short-term or long-term. Write to missionaries. Participate in a church missions conference. Pray for your missionaries. Invite missionaries to your home. Send gifts to missionaries.

Service: Be a deaconess. Work in the church library. Plan and prepare for church socials or outreach events.

Music: Sing in the choir or a special group. Play the piano. Be a worship leader. Teach children's music. Be part of an outreach team.

The church is the Body of Christ. Your local church is the most tangible representation of that body that people will see. Each one of us contributes to the building and edification of the body in some way. Some ministries seem more directly involved in evangelism and discipleship, while others appear to function more behind the scenes. But all contribute to the Great Commission God has given His church: to go to all the world with the message of Christ.

And each one of us is called by God to be available to Him to love, to share, to care — and to step into the opportunities that He provides.

10
In Your Community

The Lord Jesus makes a wonderful promise of potential ministry to us. He tells us that we will be salt in the world — He will use us to cause people to be thirsty to know Him. We will help to flavor the world with His righteousness. He also promises that we are to be light — we will shine in the darkness of a sinful world and illuminate a path to Jesus.

But with the promise, Jesus also gives a strong warning: We are not to let our salt lose its flavor and become useless. Nor are we to hide our light so that it does not shine.

Whether the community we live in is large or small, we are surrounded by people who need salt and light in order that they might enter into a relationship with the God of the universe through His Son, Jesus Christ. We're surrounded by people who hurt, who are in need, and who are looking for someone to care.

Reaching Community Women

When Patti Johnson of San Diego, California, moved into a new neighborhood, she felt it was the right time for her to look for a ministry in her community. But she didn't know what it would be or how to go about it. A week later, while at the library with her children, she was approached

by a young woman who asked her if she would be interested
in participating in a Junior Women's Club which was beginning in the area. "I took it from the Lord that I was to go,
so I told her I would be there," Patti said.

Patti spent the next year attending meetings, serving,
participating in activities and building relationships.

And then one day, as Patti relates, it was as though the
Lord said, "Patti, you've been here a whole year. They
think you're OK. I've not called you just to build relationships. I've called you to bring about change."

One area of emphasis for the club was home and family, and no one was doing anything in that area. So Patti
offered to head up a community-wide seminar called
"Heaven Help the Home" to be sponsored by the Junior
Women's Club.

"They were excited about it," Patti says. "We scheduled
it at an elementary school and printed tickets and posters
and advertised all over the community. They expected two
hundred people to come. Only about twenty showed up.
That was very hard for me. I thought I was a failure, but I
stuck with it.

"Then the next year I offered to teach a Bible study for
the Junior Women's Club. I thought maybe two or three
people would sign up, but eighteen indicated they wanted
to be a part of it."

Through Patti's Bible study several women received
Christ and Patti became something of a spiritual resource
for the club. That put her increasingly in contact with
people who were in need and women who were having
problems. Two circumstances grew out of this.

First, Patti was contacted by a woman who wanted her
to consider running for a Young Mother of the Year award.
The seminar that she did — the one she thought was a
failure — qualified her because she had been involved in
some way in building the moral fiber of the community.

Certainly no one was more surprised than Patti when she received the honor of being chosen California Young Mother of the Year. This opened many doors of ministry for her as she was asked to speak to groups throughout the state.

The second result of Patti's involvement with the women's club was meeting some battered women who needed shelter. Three or four women came at different times and lived with Patti and her family for several months each. "I saw how much their crumbled self-images needed to be rebuilt. I began to see some of the needs in our culture today. So I approached a women's resource center with which I had become acquainted earlier and asked them to teach me how to work with battered women.

"I worked there for two or three years, building relationships with many of the women, trying to minister to those who came seeking shelter," Patti relates. "Then I was asked to be a liaison between the women's shelter and community groups to obtain help from the groups. One of the community groups I was to work with was churches.

"It has been a slow process, but I've been able to involve a number of churches in reaching out to these women in need—to help them with their physical needs, to provide safety and shelter, and to meet their spiritual needs."

Patti continues to seek the opportunities that God has for her: "It all goes back to the call the Lord gave me a long time ago—that burning desire to be all that He wants me to be is still there through all these years, woven into whatever stage of life I'm in."

A New School

Jane Lillestrand was not at all pleased with the school situation that her eight- and five-year-old daughters were to enter in the fall. When she could find no acceptable alternative, she considered starting a school.

Though she had had no teaching experience other than

student teaching, Jane did have a degree in elementary and early childhood education. She had a supportive husband and she knew of two other couples who were also looking for a satisfactory educational situation for their children. With much prayer, an incredible amount of hard work, and a $5,000 line of credit, the three couples went to work. They were still looking for facilities, teachers, students and curriculum just weeks before the school year was to start.

Banner Elementary School opened that September in a rented church facility, with sixty-five students.

"Each of us adults had specific responsibilities," Jane says. "Bruce was responsible for the legal and financial affairs. My husband, Loren, was responsible for finding the teachers. Tom and Diane did many different things. Carol and I concentrated on finding students and curriculum. We all also did whatever else was needed.

"I seemed to spend most of my time on the phone. When children went down for naps, I got on the phone. I called and called and called. I usually did my housework around midnight. At school we all put up bulletin boards, we cleaned the bathrooms, we painted backdrops.

"We took the children with us everywhere. When my son Adam started kindergarten, three-year-old Judd sometimes would stay in the afternoon day-care while I worked at school."

Jane's involvement has continued over the six years the school has been in existence, but has decreased in recent years. Initially she helped to develop the kindergarten program and interviewed all the applicants for kindergarten. For a while she spent one day a week at the school visiting classrooms, observing, taking care of various details.

But when her fifth child was born, Jane backed off and was grateful for the fact that the school was running efficiently and was financially in the black.

Jane's main focus now is Bible curriculum. "We have been unable to find curriculum that emphasizes keeping Christ in the center of your lives and walking in the power of the Spirit moment by moment," she says. "We hope to supplement the curriculum we have with material which includes those important concepts and with content that is appropriate for the different age groups."

Banner has now grown to 185 students drawing from all areas of the San Bernardino and Highland, California, communities. A teacher at a local Christian high school remarked that Banner students coming in to that high school were the best prepared and the best behaved of any students that she had seen.

Jane's vision and the hard work that went with it have given her an opportunity to minister directly to her own children, and to the community as a whole.

Dinners and Discipling

The Executive Ministries' Evangelistic Dinner Party Outreach was tremendously successful in Philadelphia and many people were coming to Christ. Following up these new believers and teaching them how to walk with God was exactly the kind of challenge that Linda Wall relished.

While her husband Ron ran his two businesses and participated in the Executive Ministries follow-up on a part-time basis, Linda was able to give most of her time to following up and discipling the executive women in her area. The birth of her daughter Kelly caused her to cut back on her involvement some, but a few adjustments at appropriate places enabled her to continue most of her ministry activities. These activities fall into three main areas. The first is the basic follow-up of those who indicate they have invited Christ into their lives at an evangelistic event. This includes one-on-one appointments and speaking at follow-up coffees.

The second area is that of teaching. "Two days a week

I'm involved with the Creative Living Bible Study that we use to build those women who receive Christ. One day I participate in the training meetings for the forty-eight leaders who lead the different groups. Then the second day I actually participate in the Bible study, usually leading one of the groups. Occasionally I lecture for all 200 women."

The third area is a couples Bible study that Linda and Ron do together.

In addition, there's the paper work that needs to be done as well as individual evangelistic appointments and staff meetings on Sunday afternoons.

How does Kelly fit in to all of this activity? "Kelly is an easy child," Linda emphasizes. "If I give her something to do, she works on that. On one of the days I leave Kelly at home with a sitter. After our Bible study time I usually have individual appointments or run errands before I return home. The day of our leadership training meeting I take Kelly with me. There are several other small children there, and they play quietly together while we do our training session. I have friends who will keep Kelly on the other occasions when I might need some help, but I can usually manage to get most of my ministry done when my husband is available to take care of her.

"The Bible study takes a great deal of preparation and time, so every day when Kelly goes down for her nap, I spend an hour to an hour and a half doing that."

Why is Linda willing to put in so much time and effort in this ministry? "I love the Lord and His Word, and I love teaching. I love the studying. I love having an impact in my sphere of influence. I love helping others see what it means to trust God for the first time. I love helping people gain a vision. I am committed to launching believers into a multiplying ministry."

Upholding God's Truth

Vicky Breed has always loved to talk about Jesus. She

has boldly told many about the Lord and their need of Him. Though interested in various social issues, she had never focused on them until two events dramatically changed her life.

The first concerned Baby Doe, a newborn who because of moderate birth defects was allowed by his parents and the hospital to starve to death. "I had no idea people were letting babies starve to death. I couldn't sleep the night I heard about it," Vicky relates. "I just lay there and cried because I couldn't get rid of the thought that they actually let that baby starve to death — and that this was not an isolated case."

Then Vicky's pastor preached a sermon on abortion, quoting not only Scripture passages but describing in great detail what an abortion is like. "I had just had a baby that I had not planned," Vicky says, "and I realized how many babies, who could have come into the world as mine had, probably never made it. The reason those babies didn't live is that their mothers weren't Christians and weren't informed about abortion.

"These two incidents galvanized me into action. I could feel and identify with the issue personally. I felt that the Lord laid His hand on me and said, 'You have to do something.'

"What I did was ask my pastor if we could start a Sunday school class to pray for the nation. That's where we started."

Her class members shared information, they discussed the issues and they prayed. And Vicky began to read. She read books, she read newsletters, she read articles. She read everything she could find on the various moral issues of the day. She wanted to learn what the Bible had to say about them, to discover what was happening in society, and to discern how God's truth could be upheld.

A newspaper editorial criticizing those who mix religion and politics launched Vicky's letter-writing ministry. The letter she wrote in response to that editorial detailed the Christian history of this nation, and it was printed in full. "That excited me," Vicky says. "It thrilled me to think that I could have an influence on other people by writing, and I could do it right from my own home."

So Vicky began to write letters. Then she had opportunities to speak. She addressed the Republican Women in her community, on the subject of abortion. She was interviewed on a talk show about abortion and its implications. She has led a women's class on the effect of humanism on our society today and continues to lead the Sunday morning prayer group. She writes letters to her legislators and to the newspapers. She speaks whenever she has the opportunity—about the issues and about the biblical answers.

Vicky's main support in this ministry is her husband, Gregg. "He feels that anything one of us does is a family ministry. He encourages me to keep at it. He takes care of the kids or arranges his schedule so I can do the things I need to do. And he's always excited when I get an opportunity. It's nice to have a cheerleader."

This ministry is important to Vicki because it affects the future. "Our children are growing up in an environment that says it's all right to discard babies and even old people. I realized that my children were going to inherit a terrible, terrible legacy. That really motivated me."

Salt and Light

Whatever the community, God's children have opportunities to be salt and light:

> Sara: I had just moved to a new neighborhood, so I began to join everything I possibly could to get to know people, to build relationships, to meet needs. I asked God to open doors and provide opportunities.
>
> During this time I ran into two young Christians who wanted somebody to teach them. It was so much fun. We started at the beginning with the basics of being a child of God. They loved it, and invited one or two more. Then

at a luncheon for mothers in our neighborhood whose children were entering first grade, I announced that I was going to have a five-week Bible study on very basic, simple things about Christianity. Seven non-Christians came and it's grown to fifteen. They just keep bringing other non-Christians.

Kathy: I became involved in the PTA at my daughter's school, and I had opportunities to influence decisions concerning curriculum and school activities. And, of course, the relationships I built provided opportunities for sharing Christ.

Susie: Recently I have begun to stand outside abortion clinics to give out literature and to talk to women who are planning abortions. I encourage them not to have an abortion and to seek counseling at a Christian crisis pregnancy center.

Ginny: As I read over the textbooks my children were bringing home from their public schools, I became very concerned about the content of some of them. Obviously they were teaching things that were anti-Christian and did not uphold the moral values we felt were important.
I discovered that the textbook committees were looking for parents who would evaluate potential textbooks to help the committee decide what books would be used. I volunteered and I have had some influence on what my children and other children are learning as a result.

Patti: I went on a local campus one day a week, sharing Christ with people and finding women to disciple. Then I began to have evangelistic dinners at my home. We would invite twenty students in for dinner and share different topics, relating Christ as a part of the message.

And other mothers give us even more ideas:

With your children: Volunteer at your children's school. Be a room mother. Work with the PTA. Be available to teach special subjects at the school.

Volunteering: Work at a local museum. Participate in fund-raising drives. Join community groups and work in them. Serve at a local hospital.

Special issues: Work at a pregnancy counseling center. Picket stores carrying pornographic literature. Run for the school board or city council. Form awareness groups relating to various social issues.

Direct evangelism and discipleship: Teach a Bible study. Speak at an evangelistic dessert. Go on your local campus to share Christ. Look for opportunities to share Christ with women you work with or relate to. Tell your children's friends about Jesus. Teach in a community-wide Bible study group.

You are the salt of the earth for a people who need a thirst for all that God offers. You are the light of the world for those who walk in darkness. God has many opportunities—in your community—waiting for you to step into.

11
To Those in Need

"I tell you the truth, whatever you did for one of the least of these brothers of mine, you did for me" (Matthew 25:40).

When Jesus began His public ministry, He quoted from the book of Isaiah:

> The Spirit of the Lord is on me, because he has anointed me to preach good news to the poor. He has sent me to proclaim freedom for the prisoners and recovery of sight for the blind, to release the oppressed, to proclaim the year of the Lord's favor (Luke 4:18,19).

Even as Christ came to minister to those in need, so He has commanded us also to reach out to those in need.

"I Start to Weep"

Sharon Moore's outreach to those in need began when her husband was pastor of the Lamb's Church in Manhattan. The church had a supper club and a theater ministry to the "up and outers." But it also had a crisis care center in the building, to care for street people. And Sharon found that, as she prepared meals for five hundred people at the supper club, with her young child beside her, she was also often fixing a sandwich for a homeless person.

After a several-year break at a church in California,

97

Sharon found herself back in New York as she and her husband, Paul, together began the work of Here's Life, Inner City.

"My heart just breaks when I see the needs here," says Sharon, "especially when I look at these women who live in the single room occupancy (SRO) hotels with two or three small children. I start to weep.

"These women feed their children pop instead of milk because they have no refrigerator. They have something like $43 a week to feed a family of four or five in delicatessens and restaurants because they have no cooking facilities.

"They may have to walk down several flights of stairs," Sharon continues, "to go over to their social worker's office, and they wait in line for two to four hours to get a $2,000 to $3,000 check, which they must sign over to the hotel. If a mother wants to have her own apartment instead of one of these designated hotel rooms, the government will give her only about $400 for a family of seven.

"People are becoming aware of the problem, though," Sharon adds, "and hopefully we'll see some changes."

Sharon's involvement with Here's Life, Inner City is primarily in the area of support systems for those who are caring for people in need—like those women at the SRO's, the homeless, and the poverty stricken.

"For example," Sharon explains, "Women in Need is an organization that helps these women with housing, food, clothing, shelter, protection and education. Here's Life, Inner City helps Women in Need find the resources it requires to do the work God has given it."

A major means for linking up ministries with resources has been the "Citihope" radio program Paul and Sharon host on station WWDJ.

Each week on a live call-in show Paul and Sharon feature a different outreach to those in need in the city. As that ministry and its needs are profiled, people are able to call in and offer help.

"For example," Sharon describes, "one organization provides a place for people to come to bathe, get clean clothes, talk with a social worker, see a physician and then be sent to a church for a place to sleep. As radio listeners heard about the ministry, they could call in to offer long underwear or socks or gloves or hats or toiletries for these people. They could offer a church for them to stay in."

This same group was trying to set up a halfway house, Sharon explains, but didn't have kitchen appliances for the apartments. A Fifth Avenue apartment manager heard the program and called to say that his building was getting all new appliances and he would be glad to give the several-years-old appliances they were removing to the project.

"As you can see," Sharon says, "the return on investment is phenomenal. And this is what happens each week as we feature a different ministry."

She adds, "I probably haven't been so excited about the ministry the Lord has put in our lives in almost twenty years of being a pastor's wife as I have been with this Citihope radio program. With almost all of these ministries, the main intention is to point men and women to Christ, but we do not negate the value of touching and alleviating hunger because somebody does not profess Christ as their personal Savior. We don't ignore the human cry in the inner city just because those people don't know Christ, but we look for the opportunity to share Him."

Sharon's three children, now twenty-four, eighteen, and fourteen, have always been a part of her ministry. "They encourage me, they support me, they go along and participate whenever possible."

Sharon adds, "When the Lord allows me the privilege of looking square in the eye of somebody who is in desperate need, and touching that life, and alleviating emotional, physical and deeply spiritual needs through such simple things—I can't tell you what it does for me. It energizes me, it restores what I give out. Then I know I have been used as a vessel in the way that the Lord wants me to and that's what He asks of each one of us."

First to Volunteer

When Loveland Baptist Church in Fontana, California, began Operation Blessing to help meet the clothing and food needs of those in the community, Shirley King was one of the first to volunteer.

Shirley works part time at a mortuary and she volunteers at her seven-year-old son's school. But every Thursday morning she's at the church, sitting at the front, directing the line of people to the clothes closet or the furniture room or the food baskets, and providing the forms for them to fill out.

"I have always liked helping people," Shirley says. "You look at some of these people and you can't help but feel their needs. It's good to help, but there's just so much you can do. Often we refer them to other agencies that might be able to provide more than we can."

All the food and clothing and other items the church gives away each week are donated—by church members, or by those who receive one week and might give another week, or by other groups who give.

"Each Thursday morning the line extends down the street," Shirley says. "Those who come are given what they need until the people are all gone or what's available is all gone."

Every Thanksgiving, Operation Blessing provides chicken dinners for more than 150 families. Sometimes when they become aware of a need in the community, they seek out the person in order to meet that need. When one family's home burned, Operation Blessing was there to help provide clothing and shelter.

"It is the responsibility of the church to care for the

needy," Shirley says. "I think Operation Blessing is a wonderful program. So often people think it is a government program and they complain because they didn't get something they wanted or we ran out. We have to tell them, 'No, this is not a government program. We do this because the members of Loveland Baptist want to care for you in the name of the Lord Jesus.'"

Shirley's son, Shawn, enjoys going with her sometimes. "He is really a giver," Shirley says. "I don't know many children as generous as he is. We had a neighbor who didn't have any candy to give out at Halloween, so Shawn took his candy over and said, 'Mr. Jim, you can have some of my candy. Take what you need.'

"Often the same people return each week," Shirley says, "Many of them have been witnessed to and many have come to know the Lord through Operation Blessing. It's so good to be able to have this kind of impact in people's lives."

Ministry in Mexico

Mary Ballesteros stood before some 100 children in the detention center in Tijuana, Mexico. She told them a story about Jesus — how He could love them and could meet their needs. They listened eagerly, for many of them had no one to care for them or meet their needs.

Then she divided the kids into groups and gave them craft projects, coloring books and books to read — anything for them to do to fill the hours of nothingness that face them day after day at the detention center.

Some of the children are there for a few days, some for a few months, some for up to two years. Some have committed murder. Some have come to the United States illegally, and have become separated from their parents. The children are deported, but the Mexican government will not release them to the streets, so they are put into the juvenile system. Others are there because their parents consider them incorrigible and want to teach them a good lesson.

As the children work, Mary moves from group to group, chatting with them. "We've had many of these kids come to Christ because they are so open when they see what life in Christ can be."

Mary's ministry to the needy children in Mexico really began when she was fourteen years old. She had just received Christ and she had a definite sense that God wanted her to go to those in the greatest need. She had seen the cardboard shacks of the children in Tijuana and said, "I'm going to reach those kids for Christ." Now she says, "I truly believe it was a God-given inspiration at that point."

Mary began to learn Spanish; she became active in her church; she went on a short-term mission to Latin America; she started college and took Mexican studies. With her church she began to go to Mexico to minister.

It was on just such a trip, returning from Mexico to her home in Anaheim, that Mary met Luis Ballesteros at a church where she was sharing what she was doing in the boys' prison.

A year and a half later Mary married Luis, a Mexican citizen, and they moved to San Diego, closer to the ministry they felt God wanted them to have. Mary worked and went back to school to finish her college education. She and Luis continued to go into Mexico to share Christ and to meet needs. Two years later, five days before her son, Luis, was born, Mary's husband was killed in an automobile accident on his way home from Mexico.

Mary had to evaluate her future. A son to raise, an education to finish, and a need to support herself—but Mary was certain that God had called her to reach out to those in need in Mexico. Mary and young Luis remained in San Diego; she continued her education, and she waited. And God began to open doors.

The first door was an opportunity to go into the state prison in Tijuana one day a week and do a Good News Club with the children of the inmates there. At that time the children were kept with their parents. So once a week Mary left Luis with his grandparents in Tijuana and went to the prison.

"I found that I should be going in not only for the kids here," says Mary, "but also for the professionals, the social workers, the psychologists and the guards. They figured as an American I had everything I could want or need, so why would I voluntarily come to such a place as that state prison? What was my message that was so precious?"

So Mary discovered a ministry to children and a ministry to the women in leadership in the prison system. "God enlarged my vision, not only to include the down and out, but also people in power who can make a difference, who can open doors." It was such contacts as these that led to the opportunity for Mary to go to the juvenile detention center.

While Mary was working in the prison, the children were ordered out of the prison. She was able to have a part in helping to set up a home for these children to live in and be cared for while their parents were in prison.

Her ministry in the prison then began to expand to the women who were serving there.

"I'm working with three or four women now; I visit them once a week," she explains. "I let them know I'm there if they want to talk, and most of the time they do. They want to tell me their problems and they want me to pray for them. They ask for Christian books in Spanish."

During all of this Mary has been there for her son. When Luis was very young, Mary was able to be with him almost all the time. While she was in school, there was a nearby nursery she could use. When she began to go into Mexico two mornings a week, she was able to place him in a pre-

school where he began learning Spanish. As her opportunities grew, so did Luis, and he began attending
preschool five mornings a week.

Even so, Mary has always included Luis in her ministry. He has gone with her many times to the prison and to
the detention center. He has been able to open doors because people respond to him and remember him, so they
respond to Mary and remember her.

"He doesn't always like to go with me," Mary explains,
"and I don't want to take him all the time. But I think it's
important that he goes and sees how life is. I look back at
my sheltered background, and I know I want him to see
needs and ministry first hand. But I don't want him to burn
out. As often as possible we just take off and do something
for ourselves together.

"I figure that if I'm not there for Luis, how can I be
there for others? But it's workable to incorporate ministry
into our home life. He goes to bed at 7:00 and people can
be over and we can have deep conversations and not be dis-
turbed."

Mary feels that God has called her to this ministry and
it's up to Him to provide for her and Luis. She has some
Social Security income and has joined the Young Life staff,
raising her own support. She has a mailing list of people
who pray. "I feel that when the Lord doesn't provide for us,
that's the time we get out of ministry.

"I talk about this and it's almost like I'm talking about
someone else. It sounds like so much to do, but it's really
not. When the Lord's in it and you take it in His time, He
brings the opportunity—and it's just thrilling."

Colorado Uplift

For many years Kent and Diane Hutcheson have been
involved in evangelism and discipleship, particularly
among university students in the United States and in Asia.

After returning to the U.S., Kent, Diane and their three

young children eventually ended up in Denver to experiment with a new type of ministry. Begun as a summer jobs program for disadvantaged youth, Colorado Uplift has grown to a year-round job training program that has placed more than a thousand young people between the ages of sixteen and twenty-two in full- or part-time jobs. Kent seeks to build relationships with Uplift's outstanding executive board of leading Denver businessmen. He has led several of these men to Christ and they are making an impact in the city. He gives direction to the training that is provided in conjunction with Denver public schools, and he leads the counselors who meet with the young people.

"It is a multi-faceted ministry," Diane says. "When these kids get thrown out of their homes or get pregnant or get sick, someone has to be there for them. And, of course, part of that being there for them is to tell them about Christ."

In the first year and a half of Colorado Uplift, Kent and Diane opened their home every Sunday evening for a group of these young people from the inner city to play basketball in the backyard and to come in for refreshments, some fun and games, and a simple Bible study led by Kent. In time the kids began to open up and ask questions.

"One nineteen-year-old girl, who now serves as an office manager and secretary to Kent, trusted the Lord the first time she came into our home," Diane says. "She came from a terrible, broken background. She has had incredible struggles but today is walking with God and is really growing."

Diane tells of one young girl who shared her life story at a benefit dinner for Colorado Uplift. She told of sleeping with a guy who got her pregnant and then left. She hasn't seen him since. "But she trusted Christ in our home," Diane related. "And then she married one of the guys who had come to Christ in our program. He loved her and he loved her little baby. They now have one of their own. She has finished school and he has gone into the military. She tells everyone that 'all of this is just a result of what God can do. He's changed my life. He's given me the courage to face the future.'"

Currently Diane is discipling a group of women who are friends of hers, teaching them to share Christ and disciple others. Recently they began holding monthly professional women's breakfasts at a nearby hotel. She hopes that in the future they'll volunteer to help at the Colorado Uplift office. Many desperate needs there go unmet because the case loads are just too heavy for the regular counselors.

"Eventually," Diane says, "I believe the Lord will fit this all together. I feel the women I work with now are the kind of people who will help with Colorado Uplift."

Other Ministries

Opportunities for reaching out to those in need abound if we are willing to be available.

Elly: We have been involved in a clown group that ministers in hospitals and jails.

Gerrie: I missed nursing terribly, so I did some volunteer nursing at a base hospital. My two little ones prevented me from having a regular job, but I could do it on a volunteer basis.

Beverly: For two summers our family went with an evangelistic team to migrant workers' camps to share Christ.

Carolyn: Sometimes when I need a babysitter, I hire an unemployed woman. I meet her need and she meets mine.

Sue: Our family has been involved in ministering to an inner city family—a mother and her two children. We've had the children over to play with our children and the mother and her children over for dinner. I have shared the gospel with the mother and with the children. We also have our children give toys to the poor and money to the Salvation Army.

What could you do?

In your home: Invite those less fortunate to share a meal or share your home. Make gifts for those in need. Make crafts to sell at a fund-raising event to benefit others.

With your possessions: Give food, or clothing you or your children have outgrown, to those in need or to a church or group that provides for those in need.

With your family: Take your children to serve at a food kitchen. Help them choose toys of theirs to give to those less fortunate. Have them save to purchase gifts for other children.

As a volunteer: Give your time at a center for individuals with disabilities or a lighthouse for the blind. Collect money to benefit those in need.

With your church: Organize an Operation Blessing type ministry. Counsel at a home for abused children or abused women. Raise funds for orphan children.

When we reach out in the name of Christ to those less fortunate, to the disadvantaged, to those in need, we are truly doing the work that Christ would have us to do.

12
With Your Skills and Talents

In the parable of the talents the Lord Jesus clearly reveals the importance of being good stewards. When the master returns from his trip, he summons the servants and asks what they have done with the talents he gave them to invest. To the two who doubled their talents, he gave great praise and reward. But to the one who only buried his to keep it safe, he gave neither praise nor reward, but condemnation and rebuke (Matthew 25:14-30).

God has given each one of us specific resources for which He holds us accountable. We each have our lives, we have treasures of various kinds and amounts, we have time, and we have talents or skills or abilities or spiritual gifts. And on that judgment day He's going to ask us how we used—for His glory—what He gave us, how we invested it and multiplied it in the lives of others.

Certainly the skills and gifts that God gives us will be used to different degrees in the different seasons of our lives. But God is not wasteful and He doesn't want us to waste what He has given us.

Body and Soul

Jeanne Blocher, of Germantown, Maryland, had been teaching an aerobics exercise class for the county recreation department when her church decided to do "Body and Soul" day. There would be crafts and a Bible study, and they wanted some exercise. They asked Jeanne if she would lead it.

"My first thought," Jeanne relates, "was that I couldn't teach this class to the music that we used in my exercise classes. The Holy Spirit had already been convicting me about that type of music, but I didn't know what to do about it. I felt the exercise was good. I was taking care of myself and feeling good and helping women.

"But I had never done any choreography for dance exercise. So I borrowed some Christian albums and said, 'Lord, if You want this to be done to Christian music, You've got to do it.' In two nights' time I choreographed a whole exercise program to use with the women."

That marked the beginning of a new ministry for Jeanne Blocher. The women liked it so much that they asked if Jeanne would teach a weekly class. When her county exercise class ended, she started classes using the Christian music. Soon other women came and asked if she would train them to teach as well. When the program grew to eight classes, she put an ad on a Christian radio station. That ad brought 200 phone calls from women who wanted to exercise to Christian music with Christian fellowship.

"These really are 'Body and Soul' classes," Jeanne says. "Not only do we use Christian music, which is in itself edifying, but we always open in prayer. The spiritual emphasis of the classes varies, depending on who is in them. Some of them have a Bible study following the exercise class. When there are non-Christians in the class, we usually have a time when different ones share testimonies. Sometimes there is a prayer group after the class. Some classes are all Christian women who are looking for fellowship; others have been real outreach opportunities."

About this time Jeanne's husband, Roy, was dissatisfied in his job and began to see the possibility of "Body and Soul," with its explosive growth, actually becoming a business. With some temporary funding he was able to quit his job and began to work on the business side of the ministry. Soon it was evident that, though the business could break even, it could not support them as a family. And Jeanne always felt a conflict as to whether it was a business or a ministry.

Then came some guidance that led them to incorporate as a non-profit ministry and to begin to raise financial support for their needs. This enabled both of them to give their time to "Body and Soul" and still care for their family, and it made it possible to keep the charge for the exercise classes low so that more women could participate.

The ministry became a family affair. Their two boys have grown as the opportunities have grown. Roy and Jeanne experimented with both a couples' exercise class and a family class. "Our boys come to our family classes when they aren't in sports, and they are always praying for me," Jeanne says. "They love having the Christian music on all of the time and have begun to sing and play some instruments themselves."

Roy and Jeanne recently had a baby girl. Jeanne continued to exercise during her pregnancy, and what she learned about special modifications has encouraged many other pregnant women to exercise in "Body and Soul" classes. At one year of age, Rebecca "dances" when Jeanne turns the music on, and Jeanne is sure she will "help" with the choreography as she grows up.

"I just love being able to use my talents and skills to help others."

Musical Outreach

It started with singing at coffee houses as an evangelistic outreach on her college campus in Iowa. And she sang in church services. Then a young man who played several string instruments joined her and together they did evangelistic performances in coffee houses and on campus, and sang at weddings and community events.

After graduation they married, and Roger and Nancy Hughes continued their evangelistic music ministry on the local campus in Ames, Iowa. Their church arranged concerts or sponsored impromptu open-air musical programs. Church members would seek to share Christ with those who came to listen.

When Roger and Nancy moved to Maryland, their new church was experimenting with a unique approach to drawing people from the community and Roger and Nancy have become an integral part of that. Each Sunday morning the service starts with a half-hour concert that includes instrumental music and solos as well as choral presentations.

"This has been our main emphasis for drawing in new people, saved or unsaved," Nancy explains. "We turn the lights out and have a full-fledged concert. Then one of the elders shares a message.

"It's been a very effective format. In fact, our church has grown from about 300 last year to 600 this year."

Nancy's music ministry requires a great deal of practice, but she feels good about the arrangement they have for their four children. The church provides a legal academy for home schooling, so she is able to teach her older son at home as well as be with her preschoolers.

"I have my kids with me all day, every day, so the only time I spend away from home is on Tuesday and Saturday nights and early Sunday morning before church," Nancy says. "Because I spend so much time with the children the rest of the week, I don't feel that that is an infringement on our family life.

"We seek to make our children a part of our ministry," Nancy continues. "We sing with them, and at night before bedtime we sing to them the songs we'll be doing the next week. Our oldest is already taking violin and we hope in the near future he'll be able to participate some in our concerts.

"I think it's so important that a mother include her

children in her ministry, if not physically, at least emotionally and spiritually, so they sense they are a part of it. She needs to help them feel secure in the fact that she's really doing something for the Lord and for other people. On the other hand, I believe the family is priority and there has to be great caution so a woman doesn't go overboard as she ministers through her talents and skills."

Using Her Gifts

Donna Lynn Poland considers herself especially privileged. She has six children, covering a sixteen-year age span. She is able to use her background in psychology and teaching and her spiritual gift of serving in her primary role as mother, and to others beyond as well.

"When I did my undergraduate work in psychology, I had no idea how much I would use it. The principles that you learn just become so much a part of you. It helps me as I read various child development materials to evaluate them and say, 'Yes, that is good,' or 'No, that wouldn't work.' The principles of understanding and acceptance and building rapport that I learned in my counseling training have gone a long way in helping me to deal with my own children."

Donna Lynn also has taught at the elementary, junior high, high school and college levels. "All my teaching experience prepared me to help my own children, not only with their schoolwork, but also in their development. I'm better able to understand their learning levels and how different children learn. So now I can help them with their math, or I can help them learn to write a book report or a good paragraph or to proofread. I'm always looking for creative ways to help them in their learning process. Then as they grow older I back off and they learn to do more of it on their own."

Donna Lynn has used her psychology and teaching background to minister to others as well. Her classes on parenting have been extremely popular among young mothers. She also has taught marriage and family life classes at her children's high school in Redlands, California, and has shared home schooling of her younger children with another family.

Of her gift of serving, Donna Lynn says, "What other gift could you use more as a parent than serving? Being a parent has to be so much more than giving custodial care. So much of the joy that I've gotten from my children has been because I serve them, and I do it twenty-four hours a day. Hopefully my children are also learning to serve by seeing my example and by the service that we give each other and others."

Undoubtedly Donna Lynn's children are learning to serve by her example. Many times meal preparation for her large family has included a meal for another person in need. An excellent seamstress, Donna Lynn has sewn for her own children and for others. For children whose parents are rarely home, Donna Lynn is there to give counsel and guidance and a caring presence. And for many a young mother she has been willing to listen and to give wise advice on the other end of the phone.

"Love and Baby Powder"

"I've always been a reader," says Marilyn Barnes, "and I can remember writing short stories when I was ten. In high school I worked on the school paper and the yearbook, and at Indiana University I majored in journalism."

But Marilyn's writing involvement seemed to end then and didn't pick up again until after her second child was born. "With a friend I took a class on writing for publication and that got me back into it," Marilyn reports. "I had to write something each week, so I started writing about my experiences as a mother—some of the things I was going through and what the Lord was teaching me. By the end of that class I had sold five articles to different publications.

"Then my husband suggested I collect these little

things I had written about motherhood and put them into a book." Marilyn's initial response was, "Oh, I could never actually write a book."

Then she thought she would wait and do it when the children were older, but various friends kept encouraging her. She attended a writer's conference, and a publisher said he would be interested in her book.

"So I wrote up a proposal with a few sample chapters and sent it in. Six months later the publisher called saying they wanted to do the book. I was sitting on the bed with a can of Coke in my hand, and I got so excited I dropped the Coke!

"It took about a year and a half to write," Marilyn remembers. "Week after week I just wrote things I was going through. My quiet times with the Lord and the things He showed me from the Scriptures that related to my situation as the mother of small children provided the material. As soon as I would think I had nothing else to write about, God would bring another experience into my life."

When *Love (and Baby Powder) Covers All* came out, Marilyn was thrilled to see the book actually in print. Since then she's finding it exciting to get feedback from mothers to whom she has ministered, both in her local Denver, Colorado, area, and throughout the nation. She's heard of many women giving her book as a gift at baby showers. She receives letters and phone calls that say, "That's just what I needed to hear. I was going through the same experience."

In the midst of writing her book, Marilyn's third child was born. How did she find the time to finish the book? "Fortunately," she says, "my children were good nappers. So I could write for a couple of hours many afternoons. Sometimes I could write while they watched Sesame Street. I always did it in a rough form first, and then, when I had several of the chapters written, I would get a sitter and go to my husband's office and work all day on editing, rewriting and typing."

For other mothers of young children Marilyn says, "Go for it when you have a talent that you could use for the Lord. For me I knew it would be so much better to write while I was fresh and experiencing these things than to wait twenty years and try to recall what it was like.

"Even if you have only a couple of hours a week, it's worth it to take those first small steps toward development. Begin to grow in an area of interest and see where the Lord leads you."

Continuing in God's Call

Not long after Skip and Susan Allendorf arrived in Nairobi, Kenya, to work with the International School of Theology, Skip contracted hepatitis and went to be with the Lord. Susan, expecting their first child, returned home to have her baby.

When Amy was six months old, Susan, sure that God wanted her to continue the ministry to which He had originally called her and Skip, moved to California to the International School of Theology headquarters.

"I needed the stability of continuing to do what God had called me to do," Susan says. "Through that time God allowed me to find out more about myself and the person I was and He provided tremendous support for me."

Susan was able to work about six hours a day while Amy was cared for at an excellent child care facility. "And a couple of families included us and became like family to us. The Christian community really gave me support and encouragement and help."

Susan served as secretary to the director of the International Programs of the school. These included two overseas branches, one in Africa and one in Asia, and worldwide Institutes of Biblical Studies.

"I have always felt," Susan says, "that working in the office and having an impact on what was going on worldwide was the specific ministry God had called me to at that time. Because of the work we did, people in many parts of the world were able to hear about Christ and learn about the Bible. They could grow in their faith. Pastors, Bible teachers and denominational leaders in Africa and Asia were trained through the school to have an impact on their continents. Because of what God had called me to do in the office, they were enabled to serve more effectively. It was indirect, but it was a real ministry."

Susan has since returned to her home in Baton Rouge, Louisiana, to be near her family. During this time she has not found it necessary to work, so she can care for Amy while working on a master's degree. When Amy goes to school Susan hopes to return to teaching. Her present ministry includes teaching an adult women's Sunday school class, leading a young women's church organization, and caring for her little girl.

In addition, God has given Susan another special ministry. "In the past year God has brought across my path four young women who have recently lost their husbands. He's enabled me to write to them and to share with them my own experiences and what God has done in my life through my losing Skip. I've been able to have a specific and unique ministry."

Using Skills

Finding ways to use their skills, talents and gifts for God's glory has been important to many other moms, too.

Pamela: I did writing. I wrote training materials. I taught young adult Bible classes. I wrote books, and I did a lot of entertaining.

Carolyn: I continued to be involved with personnel work after the children were born. I helped to determine personnel procedures for a Christian organization and did evaluation of potential employees at home.

Sherry: While I've had small children, I've been able to teach classes on time management, on traditions, on

goal setting and on other subjects that are particularly
helpful to mothers.

Mary: I use my art skills with my children, at my
church, to help my husband in his work and to serve a
mission organization. My abilities have increased and
developed even as I've been home with my two pre-
schoolers.

Donna: I have taught both small groups and large
groups, developing my own questions for Bible studies. I
have also lectured to groups who would then divide into
small groups for individual study.

Ruth: I have continued to be actively involved in the
music program of every church of which I've been a member.

Susan: I do a great deal of counseling and encouraging over the phone while my children play or sleep.

What are your skills? Your talents? Your training? Your
gifts? Be assured that God has a way for you to use them.

Accounting: Provide financial counseling for your
church or neighbors. Serve on the finance committee at
church.

Art: Provide design and artwork for your church. Do
design and artwork for your children's school or preschool.
Teach a class as part of a women's program at your church.
Illustrate children's books. Volunteer to do art for a missions organization.

Cooking: Cook for church dinners. Prepare meals for
retreats. Prepare meals for those in need. Be available to
cook for evangelistic meetings. Host evangelistic parties in
your home. Help neighborhood children to bake cookies at
holiday time.

Counseling: Listen to those who need to talk. Encourage people in their walk with God. Give wise, scriptural
advice for those seeking it. Give guidance to young people
about their futures. Be available to help those with marital problems.

Crafts: Teach others how to do crafts as part of a church women's outreach. Make things to sell at a fund-raising bazaar for a missions organization or your church. Provide decorations for various church ministry programs.

Management: Organize an outreach effort for your church. Give leadership to a ministry program that interests you. Volunteer in a Christian organization. Be available as a consultant for charitable groups.

Music: Sing in a church choir. Help with the children's music program. Participate in evangelistic musical outreach. Provide solos at Christian women's clubs. Perform at convalescent homes.

Nursing: Volunteer occasionally or part time at a local hospital. Serve occasionally at your children's school. Serve at a pregnancy counseling center. Be available for minor medical advice to neighborhood mothers.

Serving: Provide meals for the ill or needy. Care for the sick. Serve behind the scenes for any church or evangelistic outreach program.

Speaking: Speak at church women's groups, Christian women's clubs, retreats. Give small devotionals for children's or adult classes. Prepare baby and wedding shower devotionals.

Teaching: Teach Sunday school. Lead children's church. Help at your children's school. Lead a Good News Club. Teach in a women's program at your church. Teach any skill you have to others who would like to have that skill.

Writing: Prepare devotionals for a church newsletter. Do a Sunday school class newsletter. Write magazine articles, newspaper articles, letters to missionaries.

Working with children: Help with Sunday school or children's church. Start a Good News Club. Assist at a preschool. Volunteer in your children's school, teaching some skill you have. Develop a puppet program.

The list could go on. Whatever your skills and talents, God has given them to you for a purpose, to use them to touch other lives. He will ask you how you have used them and multiplied them to His glory. As we are good stewards of all He has given us, we will hear, when we stand before Him, those wonderful words: "Well done, good and faithful servant. Enter into the joy of your master."

13
With Your Family

Roger and Sara Randall have always been a team in ministry. They worked on campus together sharing Christ and discipling students. When Roger directed Campus Crusade for Christ's High School Ministry, Sara gave leadership to the women in the movement. When Roger led the Campus Ministry, Sara was involved in building and motivating the women on the ministry team. When Roger has traveled to specific campuses, Sara has often accompanied him to speak and to disciple staff and students.

So it was only natural that when Allison came along she would become part of the team. In fact, Allison's first ministry began when she was three days old. A neighbor, whom Roger and Sara had led to the Lord some months before, came over to the house that evening hysterical because her cancer had returned. Roger was having no success in calming her down when Sara walked into the room with Allison. To new mom Sara's horror, the neighbor scooped Allison out of Sara's arms and began to kiss her and hug her, jiggle her and tickle her and play with her. Slowly, as she played with the child, she calmed down, and then continued to hold her for the next hour as Roger talked with her.

After the woman left, Allison threw up several times. Sara remembers telling Allison, "Allison, you really had a ministry in her life tonight. But sometimes it costs to have a ministry. You had to throw up, poor thing. But there's a jewel in your crown in heaven."

"Full On, Full Out"

At one point in Sara's life, before Allison was born, Sara had a discussion with the Lord to determine what her lifestyle was to be. After much time studying and praying, Sara was sure that God was telling her: "Sara, no matter what I do with your life, if I give you ten children or no children in the next ten years, no matter where I take you, I want your lifestyle to be full on, full out for Me. That is the overriding banner of your life. I will work out the details. I will tailor-make a special plan for you where you happen to be."

After the shock of having a baby, Sara came to the Lord again with the same question: "What is my life to be? Is there life after having a baby? Is there ministry after having a baby?"

And God reiterated to Sara the same philosophy: "Your life is to be full on, full out for Me. I will work out the details."

During Allison's first two years, Sara didn't find many opportunities for reaching out to others. But every time she did, she told Allison about her part. "I would tell her that she was having a ministry every time we had people over, whenever she had to sacrifice for something I was doing or we were doing together as a family. I told her that was a ministry and she was already having one."

That philosophy continued to permeate their relationship. Just recently, when Allison resisted being left with a sitter for Sara to teach a college Bible study at nearby Colorado University, she and her mom talked. Sara said, "You sacrifice when you let me go and tell those college girls how to have a quiet time and how to learn and grow in their relationship with Jesus. Because you do that, because you give to me, God's going to give back to you a hundredfold, plus you're having a ministry in those girls' lives." And Allison became more content.

Allison has been able to accompany Roger and Sara on many of their trips. "She considers herself on Campus Crusade staff as well. I don't think Allison would grow up to want a ministry herself if she didn't see it going on around her. But because she's been so much a part of our ministry and has seen it day by day, she's already beginning to seek her own ministry. We don't push it. But she's already told three or four of her classmates about Jesus and she prays at night for them."

The Lord's Truck

Lynda and Joe Peacock have had several different opportunities to touch lives for the Lord through the past few years. Especially significant to them is that their children have been included in those opportunities.

When Joseph and Grant were four and two, Joe and Lynda lived in California's San Joaquin Valley. One day, while they were attending a Youth With a Mission leadership school, Joe caught a vision for using the fruit that was going to waste in the valley to meet the needs of people who were hungry. He and Lynda were so excited about it that, when they returned home, they bought a tractor trailer.

"Right away the boys called it the Lord's truck," Lynda says, "and they thought it was wonderful that we were going to take this fruit to someone who needed it."

The Peacocks first took fruit to a rescue mission in Fresno. Then they discovered Mom Taylor's Pass It On Ministry in Garden Grove. Mom Taylor would take in contributions of food, clothing and furniture for refugees and needy people in her surrounding area. She used this activity as a tool for evangelism to share Christ with those people.

"We had the truck for three years, and that ministry was a real blessing for us and for our children. We would get free boxes from the packing houses. Then all of us, along with many other volunteers, would go over to the fruit sheds and pick fruit out of the cull bins and fill up the boxes. Joe worked at a cold storage plant, so we could store them there until we could haul them to Garden Grove."

Lynda and the boys usually finished their part of the project when the boxes were filled. But a couple of times they did make the trip with Joe. "It was great to see the people who needed food come in and be ministered to both physically and spiritually. We took several different kinds of vegetables and fruit—watermelon, cantaloupe, peaches, nectarines, plums, squash, carrots, everything you could think of. Many people from our church got involved. It was a real blessing for all of us."

A few years later, Joe and Lynda felt they could no longer afford to maintain the truck, but God put the burden for a similar ministry on someone else's heart.

Super Gang

After that, the Peacocks moved to Reedley, California, and Lynda found herself on a corner across the street from an elementary school. "With so many children coming by, I was sure that the Lord wanted me to start some kind of outreach, but I didn't know how. Then I met a neighbor who was having a Good News Club which she called Joy Club, and we decided to work together. She did the teaching and I led the singing. We met at our house because of its good location.

"The children really responded. Sometimes there were only eight, sometimes as many as twenty-one, usually around fifteen. My boys were six and eight at the time and they enthusiastically entered into it. They enjoyed having the other children there and hearing the stories.

"Most of the kids who came seemed to be the rowdies in school and needed a lot of love and attention. I always had a houseful of them. We soon learned to pray before they came, though, and the Lord would take control." Several received Christ at the club.

After the first year, Lynda had the club, now called Super Gang, by herself. One of the special things they did was to visit a nearby convalescent home. "The children sang and visited with the residents. Everyone loved it. We received a blessing and so did the older people.

"Joseph and Grant were totally involved in all of this. Sometimes all the kids would ride bikes to visit some elderly friends in different parts of town. We would sing and talk with the people. One little boy lost his mother, and we went to sing for him and his dad. That was a really special time."

When the Peacocks moved back out into the country, their kids said, "Aren't we going to have Super Gang anymore?"

"They really loved it," Lynda says. "I think it has helped them to have more understanding and consideration when people who are not very lovely have come into their lives. They saw people from broken homes and people who weren't getting much love. They learned to put up with people who were hard to get along with. Now I see that both of them have compassion for people — they really care. Both are considerate of the elderly, and I'm sure that goes back to the years when we went to the rest home."

Since moving to the country Lynda and Joe have been home schooling their boys and have found opportunities for ministry as a family to be less formal and more spontaneous. Joe taught their boys and three others an industrial arts class. "The home schooling has pulled us all closer together, allowing more time for each other. We minister to each other, we visit people who have needs, and we open our home for fellowship and for people who need a place to stay for a few days or weeks," Lynda says. "We want to be open to whatever God shows us to do as a family."

"We Are a Team"

In their time with Campus Crusade for Christ, Swede

and Judy Anderson have lived in Texas, Arizona, Pennsylvania, California, Mexico and Washington, D.C. Their children have grown up in a variety of living, cultural and ministry situations. Their youngest is now in college and all three of the children love the Lord and seek to serve Him.

One significant contributor to the depth of their spiritual lives is the fact that Swede and Judy have always made their children feel they are a part of their ministry.

"The children have opened up so many opportunities for us to share the Lord and the gospel with couples, with families and with their friends. We've been able to minister together with them," Judy says, "and thus train our own children in how to lead their friends to the Lord.

"We have told our children consistently over the years that we are a team. Each one is supportive of the others. They've grown up with the understanding that, when Swede is in some other city doing something, he is a part of us and we have a part in his freedom to go. We pray for him. We are a part of what he is doing.

"We often have people into our home," Judy relates. "We've had non-Christians, and the children have sat at the table with us as we have talked with these people about the Lord. We have had people who have walked with God for many years, and the children have heard how God is faithful in these people's lives. They've met and talked with heroes of the Christian faith and with scholars — and with skeptics."

Swede and Judy also have tried to include the children in their travels. Often they have spent money to enable Swede or Judy to take one of the children on a trip with them rather than spending money on other things that might be more tangible.

"We've encouraged them to keep in touch with children they have met in different parts of the world through our various ministry opportunities. This keeps them more aware of children from different backgrounds who are growing with the Lord."

A special area of ministry in which Swede and Judy have included their family has been that of giving. "We have always given, but we've always set aside a portion of our offering each month to accumulate to meet a special need. When a person has a particular need or there is a specific ministry opportunity, we can become partners with the children in helping meet the need."

Through the years God has used others to give so many benefits to them, things such as clothing, furniture, cars, and special trips and privileges for the children, that Judy says, "In turn we want to do the same for others. When we're not using something, or if there is something a friend has really admired, we often give it away.

"Sometimes this has meant sacrificing and cutting corners for us. But I think it has influenced our children. They are very generous. They are satisfied materially. We have lived in communities where the people around us have much more than we do, but our children have not resented it or felt a need to compete. They seem to understand that what we have is from the Lord and we have much to be grateful for. At the same time they have a willingness to give and to include others in their lives."

Ministry a Family Affair

For all God's children it is possible — and needful — to make ministry a family affair.

Susie: I take my children with me to visit elderly, lonely neighbors. We sometimes make food to take and even my four-year-old helps. The children carry our presents to whomever we're visiting. I hope they're learning to give of themselves, to communicate with older people, and to understand that not everyone is young and healthy. I've also encouraged the children, by word and example, to be quick to write notes to people in need. We encourage them to look for the person who appears to be left out and to reach out rather than feel they have to be in the "in" group themselves.

Ginger: I lead an exercise Bible class and my children attend with me. My older son helps me set up and I tell him what a special helper he is. He looks forward to going each week so he can be my helper. I also pray with my children and share requests with them.

Beverly: I take the children visiting with me and we often make cookies or cards for people. In letters and thank-you notes to unsaved friends and family, the children include their usual array of stickers, and these carry a message. We also seek to pray for others as a family.

Donna Lynn: I have a speaking ministry and my children often accompany me and play the handbells. They also help with puppet shows that I give. They write letters and draw pictures for many people who are in the hospital or discouraged and lonely. They pray with me for specific people. And they help me with ideas as I write Bible curriculum or counsel others.

Fran: When Dad goes to share Christ with someone, the children and I stop to pray. They are just learning to share with their own friends. When I directed a children's choir at our church, one boy often helped me put books on the chairs and get the treats out at the end. We also have had backyard clubs in our neighborhood and our children have gone out and invited their friends.

Bonnie: Hospitality has been an important ministry for us. Around our home the word "guest" is a synonym for good times. Our kids have helped us set the table for company and often have a part in preparing for our guests. Our children have a ministry also as those who come from difficult backgrounds are able to observe a Christian family.

Natural Ministry

Our children can so easily be a natural part of our ministry.

In our homes: When we show hospitality, they might have to give up their room or adjust their schedule or forego a TV show. They can help prepare a meal and set a table.

To the ill: Cards and notes can be such an encouragement. Our children can often say something to an unsaved person or a needy person that would not be acceptable from an adult.

Visiting the lonely: Children can have a tremendous impact in the lives of the elderly or those who are alone for some other reason. They often benefit as much as the one to whom they minister.

By praying: Their ministry will be far reaching when they pray for those who have needs, for those who are suffering, for friends and relatives who don't know Christ. And they will gain a heart for bringing people before the throne of grace.

Making gifts: This is probably one of the most popular ways for children to reach out and encourage, to say "I love you," and to touch a life for Christ.

Going along: When we share Christ, when we counsel, when there is a disciple to meet, our children can observe, play quietly and pray. They often open doors, and they can see God working.

With their friends: Your children can bring into your home neighborhood children who would otherwise go home after school to an empty house. Children can befriend those who are not so popular. Encourage your children to share Christ with their friends or to invite them to Sunday school.

Truly the family is the key to a healthy society for future generations. Our children are our most important disciples. If they are to grow into an understanding of what it is to be available to God, to step into opportunities to touch lives for Him, they must see it in our lives and they must have a chance to participate with us.

14
To the World

The Great Commission that the Lord Jesus gave us was to go to all the nations, to the uttermost parts of the world, to preach the gospel and make disciples (Matthew 28:18-20). And God has given just such a ministry—to the uttermost parts of the world—to some mothers.

Breakfast Outreach

For Barbara Jakob, a ministry grew out of the study group for young mothers that she began in her Zurich, Switzerland, home (see page 69). Recognizing that women had many needs and questions but few answers for their lives, Barbara initiated her first "Breakfast for Women by Women."

She and her discussion group invited hundreds of Zurich women to breakfast at a large hotel to hear a prominent speaker "share the good news in a modern way—to help them find solutions to their problems." They prayed for 250 to attend. Five hundred came. That was just the beginning.

Many of the women who attended joined a discussion group. Many eventually came to Christ. More breakfasts were held. The results multiplied, first in Zurich, then throughout Switzerland, as other women caught a vision for reaching out to their peers.

When Barbara and her family moved to Germany, she began to hold breakfasts and discussion groups there as well, and she is now reaching out for Christ in twelve German cities.

"The movement has spread to eight European countries in more than forty cities," Barbara reports. "All the breakfasts—several each year in most cities—have an attendance of 200 to 1,000 women. Just in Switzerland there are now more than 400 discussion groups. We have had requests for help in establishing groups in Thailand, Canada, South America and the United States."

This rapidly growing outreach has led to two books and numerous magazine and newspaper articles, as well as television coverage for Barbara. "This has been the most mind-blowing thing that could happen to me as an ordinary mother," Barbara emphasizes. "I know that God's hand is in all of this, and without the mighty work of His Holy Spirit it could not have happened! I am astonished—and humbled—that God uses me in spite of all my mistakes and faults."

Called as a Family

Vonette Bright's ministry has certainly been to the whole world. She has traveled with her husband, Campus Crusade for Christ founder Bill Bright, to many countries. She has spoken, she has shared Christ, and she has led prayer conferences throughout the world. But when her children were young, her outreach to the world was done from her home.

In fact, the world has often come to her home. Vonette was a home economics major, and providing a comfortable atmosphere for people to visit and learn about Christ has been one of her primary ministries. People from many different parts of the world have met Christ at her hearth or have grown closer to Him in the warmth of her home.

Since Bill traveled so often, Vonette looked for ways to

include the children in his worldwide outreach. "When they were very young I would send tapes to Bill, having the children tell Daddy what we had been doing.

"Bill always brought something back to the children. I would set a clock with the time where Daddy was in the world. We would read from the encyclopedia and look at the map to learn about the country he was visiting.

"Of course, we prayed for Daddy, too. He would give us a report on what happened when he returned. We both wanted the children to share in the fruit of the ministry, in the good things that happened. We stressed that God had called us as a family to serve Him. It was especially wonderful that, when Daddy went away, it was not to make money, but to serve God."

As the children grew, they were consistently exposed to Campus Crusade for Christ training. They had opportunities to travel with their parents as well and to see the world for themselves, to see the needs in the world, and how Christ could meet those needs.

"Husband-Supported Missionary"

It is not necessary, though, to go to the world to be a "world Christian." Sandy Shelby, of Lynwood, Illinois, relates, "I have always had a missions burden. I wanted to be a missionary myself, but my health prevented it. The Lord closed that door, but our family had always tried to be world Christians before we ever heard that title."

Sandy considers herself a "husband-supported missionary" now, with a far-reaching ministry to the entire world. She has served on numerous missions committees in the various churches they have attended and currently is a consultant to the women's missions program at her church. Her efforts to broaden the church's missions commitments include planning tours of mission centers and organizations in the States, month-long missions emphasis programs at her church, and luncheons at which missionaries speak.

"I also work on a banner committee. We make six-foot banners of missionary board logos and whenever any of our missionaries come into town, we display the banner for their mission board. So far, we have about sixteen banners to represent our missionaries."

Sandy and her husband, Jim, have recently applied to become local representatives for World Radio Missionary Fellowship, the parent organization of HCJB radio in Quito, Ecuador. They will represent the organization in their area, seek to promote it, provide housing and transportation for missionaries visiting the area, and help in any way possible to support the efforts of that mission group.

The Shelbys' commitment to missions is a family affair. "We often have missionaries over for dinner or to stay overnight in our home. The children not only get to meet them and become involved in their lives, but they also have a part in serving them by cleaning the house and preparing the meals.

"We have always taken our children with us to missions conferences, missions concerts, and missionary society meetings. They sit quietly. They don't always enjoy all of it, but they are learning to have a heart for missions and for the world."

Since her children are home schooled, Sandy has found it especially important to involve them in church missions activities so that they can relate to the other children. "We always have something for the kids at our missions conferences, and ours always enter the poster contest or the reading contest. We tell them we're not concerned whether or not they win, but we just want them to reach out and get involved in ministry."

"The Packettes"

An important family ministry has earned the Shelbys the name "the Packettes."

Sandy says, "We help missionaries who are going to the field to pack their belongings. As a family we go to their home with some banding material and pack them up. Most of these new missionaries know nothing about packing, but we've developed a system. We have a scale that we use because each box needs to weigh about sixty-eight pounds. They need to be full without one square inch of airspace. It's like we're working a big jigsaw puzzle.

"We've also trained some other families in our church to do this because there is such a need. So often missionaries are really under stress by the time they get to packing, having spent time going through training and deputation. They might even still be struggling with 'Does God really want me to do this?'

"A husband may be saying, 'I need every one of those theology books,' but there's not enough room to get even all the essentials in. This has been a very exciting ministry for our family."

World View

In order to help her children prepare for a possible call to the mission field, Sandy has encouraged each of the children to learn to play a portable musical instrument. Nancy and Melinda play the flute and Danny is learning the guitar. Even in learning their instruments they have the world in view, for the Shelbys choose teachers who will require the children to use their musical skills in ministry as they are learning.

Now that their children are older, the Shelbys have seen some of the fruit of their lifelong emphasis on reaching the world. Their daughter Nancy recently went on a six-week mission project and has returned with a desire to go into full-time Christian service. Melinda spent last summer working at a Bible conference center. Sandy couldn't be more pleased.

Other Ways to Reach Out

Many other women have found ways to reach out to the uttermost parts of the world:

Jill: Our family went on a short-term missionary project for church planting in Italy. While there the children occasionally went with us to street meetings where they passed out tracts. It was good for them to learn what it is to sacrifice a bit for the cause of Christ.

Elizabeth: When we were living in Singapore I found someone to keep my toddler one afternoon a week and I went to the university campus to share Christ. My husband and I were able to win and disciple nine key students, all of whom eventually went into Christian work.

Eine: In serving Christ throughout Europe, we have taken our children with us to meetings, conferences and foreign countries as often as possible. They have lived with us in our ministry twenty-four hours a day. They have shared our joys and our sorrows, prayed with us during the hard times and seen the miracles that God has done in individual lives. They have helped us plan our ministry, write prayer letters, stuff and mail prayer letters, and raise support.

Sandy: We have a bulletin board in our hall with pictures of missionaries. This way the whole family can see them and pray for them on a regular basis. We also have artifacts and decorative items that missionaries have given us and, as we see these or pick them up to dust them, we pray for those missionaries.

Bonnie: While we were living in Germany I was able to exercise hospitality liberally. A myriad of meal-time or overnight guests came into our home and provided us with opportunities for caring and serving.

The world is great and greatly in need. The opportunities are manifold.

Through your church: Participate in a missions conference. Help to build a missions display booth. Attend discussions with missionaries. Invite a missionary into your home. Bring together high school and college young people to meet with and get to know missionaries.

With your family: Adopt a missionary family. Pray for them. Prepare and mail their prayer letters for them. Write letters to them. Encourage your children to get to know the children of your missionary family. Have a missions bank for your family to put small change into to contribute toward reaching the world. Encourage your children to babysit for missionaries and Christian workers as a ministry. Provide cross-cultural experiences, such as attending a foreign-language-speaking church, for your children. Go on a short-term missions project as a family.

While living overseas: Reach out to neighbors. Host an evangelistic coffee in your home. Start a children's Bible club. Gather some friends for prayer. Seek to befriend other foreigners living in the country, as they are often without friends and lonely. Become active in a local church. Look for opportunities to minister to military personnel in that country. Practice hospitality.

The Great Commission is for each one of us. And whether or not we ever leave the shores of our country or our home environs, God encourages us to reach out to the uttermost parts of the world.

15
As a Way of Life

Recently I visited my good friend Carla Kliever, whom I hardly ever see, for three wonderful days at her home in Reedley, California. The highlight of the visit was observing the way-of-life ministry God has given Carla and Howard and their children.

The first night I was there "Sandy" came by. She was having trouble handling a situation regarding her ex-husband and her children, and Carla spent an hour talking and praying and reading Scripture with her.

While Carla was talking with Sandy, Howard got a call from "Tony." He needed some help in getting a message to Howard and Carla's neighbors. Howard went out at 10:30 at night to deliver that message.

The next day I listened as Carla counseled with a woman on the telephone. That evening "Rosie" came by. She was having marital problems and needed someone to listen and pray with her. Carla was available.

At church, Carla told about a family with whom she and Howard had been sharing Christ. The wife was eight months pregnant and the husband had injured his foot. They needed to move the following weekend. Could the church help? Immediately four hands went up—men who would go over on Saturday and help them move.

The next evening Carla's next door neighbor knocked on the door with her two small children. Her husband was away, she was pregnant and hadn't been feeling well and just "had to get out of the house." We spent the next two hours chatting with her.

Spontaneous Availability

Ever since I've known Carla she's been involved in reaching out to others. In the past her ministry had been more often in structured, formal, planned situations. How had this spontaneous, way-of-life ministry come about in Carla's life?

"I was teaching full time and Howard was busy in his job and our lives belonged to other people, but I began to wish that I weren't so locked in and could live more of a spontaneous life," Carla begins. "God was giving me a desire just to be somebody's neighbor with whatever that might entail. Howard has always been poised for spontaneous ministry. He's like that. I've been the one who wanted to sit down and plan and make lists. But God was beginning to prepare us.

"Howard lost his job; I had another baby and quit teaching; and the Lord brought it all together. The flexibility of Howard's work now, the kind of house we have, the kind of church we're in, even the town we're in and the location of our home contribute to our spontaneous lifestyle. The contrast between the rat race we used to live and what we live now, which is so much more easy-going and spontaneous, is unbelievable."

Much of this was already beginning to happen when a fire destroyed a large portion of Howard and Carla's house. "We've always wanted a big house and we've always wanted a house that would lend itself to Bible studies and home fellowships and guests and children. So it was great that, after our house burned, we were able to redo the floor plan with ministering from our home as a main thought. We designed the house to better fit the kind of life God was giving us.

"The day of the fire we put a big sign on the front of our house that said 'This does not change our love for the Lord Jesus Christ.' That started many people talking about the Lord with me," Carla recalls.

A few weeks later a neighbor asked Carla if she would lead a Bible study. So this new Christian opened her home and Carla went to teach. Every Wednesday morning "ladies would come walking up the street from different ends of the block carrying their Bibles. It was a chance for me to get very direct about the claims of Christ as expressed in the book of John."

One woman in the neighborhood drops by from time to time just to talk, and the conversation often turns to the Lord. "She comes down and starts to share her marriage problems, and I tell her from a biblical perspective what I think should be done. I find myself saying more and more to people I counsel to find what God says and do what God says, to go to God, to read the Word."

A Supportive Church

Carla's church, with the support it offers, is a major contributor to making possible the kind of ministry she and Howard have. "There are ministries in our church that are helping to meet physical, social, emotional and financial needs. So it doesn't matter who comes to me with a problem, I know I'm not alone in facing that problem with them. I've got a whole body of people and resources available. If a counseling situation is above my head, or if it's an area I don't feel competent in, I know there is someone in our church, the pastor or one of the elders or another member, to whom I can send this person. I've never before been in such a secure situation in terms of body ministry."

The church has a clothing warehouse, a food pantry, a crisis pregnancy clinic and a 24-hour prayer chain. "We're always being taught by the pastors and elders that Christianity is serving. That's what we and the others in our body are seeking to do.

"If there is a need that we can't meet since our church is a small body, then we send the people to another good church in the area that could meet that need. That's a good witness — to the whole community — of the unity of the body of Christ in our city.

"But I believe God really wants us to pour our time and money, and our counseling and teaching, into those who have expressed a desire to be a part of our own church family. So when someone from my church or who has in some way become involved in our body is on my doorstep, I feel like I'm commanded by the Lord to give them my time, my ear, my food — whatever it is that they need."

Though her emphasis is on reaching those in her own body, this has given Carla more opportunities to reach people who need the Lord, who are completely unchurched, than she's ever had before. "Our neighborhood is full of people who have very concrete needs for the Lord."

An important part of such a way-of-life ministry is knowing when to stop, when to put your foot down. Carla says she finds herself saying sometimes, "I've already told you what I know the Lord wants you to hear. There's nothing more I can do for you. I've helped you in every way I can. You need to do what God says."

For Carla one of the highlights of this kind of life is that it is a total family ministry. She and Howard are able to do it together. They have been told by others in their church that they have the gift of hospitality. Amy and Laura, their two daughters, are equally a part of it.

"That's another confirmation that this is the kind of life God wants us to have. Our children are so used to company and to having people just drop by that I can say, 'Let's put things away,' or 'Please help me set the table,' and the kids just pitch in. When children come, they take them out to the back yard or up to the playroom and play with them.

"When there's a heavy counseling time," Carla emphasizes, "sometimes I have to juggle who needs me the most, the person or my children. Usually I can get my children occupied or make some arrangements for them. I try not to extend them too much as I seek to meet other people's needs.

"But this is such a perfect way to help my children see their need for Christ by how He meets needs in others' lives. I want them sheltered from sin and from the harmful things of this world. But I want them prepared to live in the world. What better way is there to show them the difference between the kingdom of God and the kingdom of the world than to let them see it lived out in people's lives? They hear us praying for people. They pray with us for people — for marriages that need to be mended, for physical healing, for spiritual needs, for financial needs.

"I think, as the children are involved in ministry within a secure and structured environment and yet still exposed to people who are hurting, people who are paying the consequences of their sin and wrong choices, the children will learn to trust God and to make the right choices for themselves.

"You should never throw your children or your husband out for the sake of the ministry," Carla stresses. "They must come first and everything else must be an extension and a family project. But I'm so grateful that God has made our home into a refuge, a stopping point, a lighthouse to show the way to people who need the Lord."

"Lord, Send Someone Today"

As Anita Cleary left her singles celebration class one Sunday, a woman said, "Hi, Anita. How are you?" And then the woman started to cry. She had some things on her mind and needed a friend to talk to. "So we talked for a while," Anita remembers, "and we prayed about it, and she walked away with a smile on her face."

"One of my prayers every morning is that someone who

needs to hear about the Lord or is prepared to hear what I have to say or who needs some kind of special encouragement will walk into my life. And the Lord has really answered my prayers in abundance."

Anita became a Christian as a young child but drifted far from the Lord. After a divorce and the need to care for her young child alone, she found herself returning to Him. Through her church she found someone to disciple her and to build her in her faith, and God has given her a desire to reach out and tell others about Christ and to help them grow.

Her San Diego home is often open to others, and a care group has met there regularly. Friends feel free to come by and chat. Anita particularly feels a burden for the children of single parents and is seeking ways to include them in the family life of the church and the singles group.

One evening she went to her ex-husband's home to pick up her son, and she encountered some of her friends from previous days. They were very antagonistic to her newfound faith. Yet when she started to leave, one of the women asked her to drive her home since she was intoxicated and unable to drive.

As they were driving, "Sally" asked Anita if she could spend the night at her house and Anita said yes. During the entire trip home Sally carried on a terribly negative conversation. As they arrived at Anita's and began to make up the hide-a-bed, her friend was abrupt and angry. Then suddenly "she threw herself onto my couch, folded her arms, looked at me and said, 'Now tell me about Jesus.'"

For the next two hours Anita and Sally talked about the Lord. "She really bombarded me. If I'd been a Christian for twenty years, I couldn't have answered the questions fast enough. She was so hungry and the answers just flew out of my mouth. There's no way I was coming up with the answers. It was the Holy Spirit. After we talked, we cried together and we prayed together. Since then Sally has gone through some rough times, but she is back in church, and she and her husband have reconciled. They have a common bond now."

Anita's son is always a part of her ministry. When the care group meets at her house, he's there and plays quietly and listens. When Anita is being discipled, Adam again is responsive to allow Anita to have that time with her friend and with God. "He is very patient and we talk a lot about what I'm learning and what I'm going through. He is my most important ministry. Through him I've also been able to reach out to some of the mothers of his friends at school. The Lord has given me boldness I never thought I'd have.

"I used to find myself praying, 'Lord, please don't let me have to share now. I don't want to witness to this person,'" Anita admits. "But the opportunity arises and I know this is it whether or not I'm comfortable with it. I have to let God take over and let Him work through me.

"I feel that He has given me a beautiful vision early in my Christian life to see the opportunities out there and the joy we can have when we get involved and open our lives up to Him."

A Letter From Home

Myra Gilchrist certainly has had a ministry as a way of life. Now living in San Bernardino, California, Myra still has an impact on lives in her former Oregon home. Read what one friend wrote to her about the effect that Myra had on her life:

"Except for my mother, there is no doubt that you have influenced my life more than any other person. I am always quoting you and using you for an example.

"You always make time and put yourself out to be hospitable to everyone. You are such a good manager of your own time that you always have time to help heal the hurts and meet the needs of others.

"You did so many nice things for your family and friends, all the extras that made your home so special, and you weren't even aware of how much more you did and gave of yourself than most people do. I know you really have the heart of a servant and that is really God's heart in you.

"One amazing thing about your four kids that has impressed everyone who knows them is how good they are. Your kids were always obedient, well-behaved and respectful. I think you had happier times together because of the harmony that was present.

"I know your kids were usually a part of any group in your home. I realize now that young children who are exposed to this kind of lifestyle tend to claim that same quality in their own lives. I don't know how you were so spiritually mature at such a young age. I know you had your children pray with you for decisions in your life. It made them part of your prayer team and let them recognize God's answers as they came. The result in your family is an outstanding testimony to all they meet.

"If I could have people describe me, I would like them to say I had integrity, compassion and forgiveness — or to say I reminded them of Myra."

Way of Life

Sometimes we will be involved in formal ministry. Sometimes we will have structure to our outreach. But always, everywhere we go, all of us should be involved in ministering, in being available to step into the opportunities to touch lives for the Lord as He provides. For a mother, those opportunities are going to come most often as a way of life.

> Donna Lynn: Don't use children as an excuse for ministry being ended. See them, instead, as the beginning of a much broader and deeper ministry. It's twenty-four hours a day for them. It's a ministry in all the new areas of life they bring — pediatrician's office, schools, library, neighborhood play, discussions with other mothers.

Sandi: When we lived in New York, we had a Good News Club in our home. Some Jewish children came and received the Lord. I always believed in our home being a Grand Central Station for the neighborhood kids. You know, "Today is brownie-baking day or cookie-baking day and we'll send those home with the kids."

Diane: One morning recently I went to a neighborhood coffee, almost regretting the time it was taking, but feeling I needed to meet more of my neighbors. That morning I met a young Vietnamese wife who had two children in my children's school. What a story she had! We agreed to get together, and as we slowly went through the message of Christ, she invited Him into her life.

It is thrilling that something we think may not be the most important—if we're really seeking for God to use our time to the fullest—God often turns into a significant encounter. I find it vital to look for opportunities in our natural commitments. On one of my daughter's gymnastic trips, one of the mothers trusted Christ with me. We are getting to know parents on the soccer team and we hope to have them over for a dessert at Christmas time.

Ann: Occasionally God gives me an opportunity while I'm shopping or running errands to share briefly that I'm a Christian and give a tract. I find that when people come to do a service at our home, I can share a little bit about my faith in God.

Marilyn: I find I can share with a girl in a restaurant, a young man at a laundromat, the people we helped after their truck overturned on the interstate. God brings people across our path no matter where we are.

Julie: Each week as my son was in tumbling class, I chatted with another mother. Slowly we became friends. Her husband was of another faith and she had no faith. But that didn't stop our friendship from developing. Our families have done many things together over the past two years. Our children enjoy playing with each other. We keep each other's children from time to time. She has attended Christian events with me, and she's heard the message of Christ. She has not received Christ as yet, but

I'm going to keep loving her and keep being her friend. Hopefully someday she'll be my sister in Christ as well.

Can everyone have a ministry? Can everyone see God use them? Every mother? Certainly.

In the neighborhood: Be a friend. Introduce yourself to that new neighbor. Listen to that lonely lady down the street. Take a meal to the sick family across the way. Open your home to the neighborhood children and to their parents. Look for opportunities to share about the one who gives you the love to be that kind of friend.

Through your children: Attend their sporting events. Help at their school activities. Be a friend to their friends. Talk with other mothers at the park.

In your church: Offer counsel to that young mother in need. Listen to the young couple with financial problems. Encourage the elderly lady who sits in the same pew with you. Phone those who are shut-ins.

As you travel: Find out about your seatmate on a plane or train or bus. Discern their needs and interests. Share about yourself, including what Christ means to you. If there is interest, tell them how they can know Christ in a personal way. *Everywhere you go:* At the doctor's, in the grocery store, at the gas station, in the park, on the beach, at an amusement park, to a service person. Give a smile; say a kind word; ask about them; share the love of Christ when you can.

In Colossians 1:28 the apostle Paul proclaims, "Everywhere we go we talk about Christ to all who will listen" (TLB). Everywhere we go, the way we live, what we say, how we treat our children, how we reach out to people, what we do with our time—each of these will be a witness, a testimony, a ministry. As we are filled with the Spirit of God and totally available to do all that He wants us to do, He will lead us to opportunities, moment by moment, day by day, to reach out and touch someone for Him.

16
Some Significant Help

Significance. You are a significant person. God has created you that way. There is great significance to your mothering. And there is great significance for you, your children and your world as you become an increasingly caring, outreaching and ministering person.

But how do you begin to make the right choices? You certainly can't do all—or even many—of the things suggested in this book. Probably one or two ideas will be all you can pursue at any one time. How do you know what you should be doing, what you should emphasize? In this chapter I'd like to offer you some help in the areas of choosing priorities, scheduling your time, managing your home and caring for your children.

Choosing Right Priorities

All our choices must begin with right attitudes and right relationships. Our first priority must be our relationship with God. There needs to be a total commitment to God—that complete availability to do whatever He wants us to do, to go wherever He wants us to go, to be whatever He wants us to be, as we talked about before. We must come to God and say, "I submit myself to you. I want to be the person You created me to be. I want all that You have for me, but only what You have for me."

When we've made that kind of commitment and truly seek His choices for us, then it's important that we look closely at ourselves. We need to evaluate who we are, what we're like, and what we're able to do in light of the circumstances of our life at this time. You've just read the stories of more than thirty women and how God is using them. Dozens of other mothers have shared ideas, too. If you're like me, you often found yourself saying, "That's a great idea"; or "I wish I could do that"; or "Maybe I could try that." It is my prayer that you would get many ideas from these other mothers as they've shared their lives and hearts with you.

At the same time, we must resist the temptation to compare ourselves to others. Each of us is unique and individual. Each has specific strengths, different energy levels, a variety of gifts and her own particular family situation. Some of us can run three-ring circuses and some of us can barely handle one ring. One woman's husband might be very supportive of her efforts to reach out, while another's could be antagonistic toward anything she does outside the home. Some of us are blessed with healthy children, while others seem to live at the doctor's office. One mother might have one peaceful, sleeping baby while her friend has three extremely active preschoolers. It is extremely important that we recognize who we are and what is reasonable — with God's strength — for us to consider as possibilities and opportunities.

Discerning God's Goals

Then, with an attitude of total availability and a reasonable understanding of our own abilities, we can ask God to show us what He wants us to do. We should consider what God would want for us in the long-term future as well as for the immediate events of our lives. Of course, part of His future plans for us include the specific things that God has said should be true for all of His children: We're to become more like Jesus. We're to be His disciples. We're to tell people about the Lord Jesus and help them grow in Him. We're to glorify Him in all that we do.

God has individual plans for us as well. I find it helpful to imagine that I am blowing out the candles on my eightieth birthday cake. As I look back over my life, what kind of memoirs would I like to have for myself? What kind of person did I want to become? What would I like to have accomplished in my life?

These long-range goals help me to choose better specific, short-range goals that move me in the direction I believe God wants me to go. For example, some ideas from this book could well be included in short-term goals for the next six to twelve months of my life.

Think for a moment of the possibility of adopting one of the ideas you have read about here. Perhaps in ministry to your family you would like to develop a particular character quality or skill in your child. Or you want to see the spiritual atmosphere of your home improved. Do you feel a need to plan a regular family time? Maybe you'd like to discover an opportunity for ministry beyond your family. Perhaps you want to get involved in some outreach program in your church. Possibly you could use your home to reach out to children in your neighborhood. Is there a concern in the community that you could help resolve? Perhaps a ministry of prayer would fit your life at this time.

What possibilities in each area of ministry — to your family and beyond your family — does God seem to be revealing to you? Which would be the top priority idea for ministry to your family? Which would be the top priority for ministry beyond your family? Take a minute right now to get a 3 x 5 card or your planning notebook or some paper. Write down the top priority activities you believe God is leading you to pursue.

The next question is, How? How will you accomplish what you believe God wants you to do? What steps or activities will take you the farthest toward the goals you have set? What would be the first step you need to take — even in the next day or two? What steps would you need to take after that? Do you need to do some research, take a class, read a book, get some training, hold a family conference, make a phone call, or purchase some equipment? The Resource List in the appendix can provide many sources for help in determining how to get started. When you have identified those first steps you need to take, write them on your card.

Now tape that card to your mirror, on your refrigerator door, or by your sink — someplace where you will see it every morning. We are much more likely to follow through on our plans if we keep them before us.

Scheduling Your Time

All the best plans, the best intentions, the best "to do" lists will be meaningless if they don't make it into your day-to-day schedule. Is it really possible for a mother with young children to schedule her time effectively? I believe it is. Let me suggest an approach that works — if we remain flexible. Then I'd like to share with you an adaptation of this plan that was especially helpful to me when my children were very young.

Pick a morning, any morning — maybe tomorrow. Pull out — or make out — your "to do" list. Undoubtedly there will be more things to do than you can do in one morning.

Ask yourself, Is there someone else who could do any of these? Is your husband available? Is a child old enough to assume some responsibilities? Do you have a friend who could help you? Ask that person to take that item.

Next, determine which remaining activity is the most important thing you can be doing. Which is your number one priority? Could it be the first step toward one of your ministry ideas? Which is number two?

Then, write into your schedule what you are going to do. How much time will it take to do that number one activity? Put that into your schedule. How much time will it take to do the next? Write that into your schedule. Be sure to allow some flex time, recognizing that things probably will not go quite as you have them planned.

This approach to time scheduling will work for a month, a week, or an hour, whatever time allotment you choose. But how can you make sure you follow your schedule? The secret is always to be doing your number one priority.

We are so often tempted to get all the little things out of the way before we start on our priority activity. Usually that means that all those little things get in the way and we don't get to the most important thing.

Of course, your priority can change, even momentarily. The activity you listed as number one may be the most important thing for tomorrow morning, until your child has a need that can't be postponed. That would then become number one. Maybe you're working on something creative, and you need a break. The break becomes your priority then. When noontime comes and you need to fix lunch for your children, that becomes your number one priority. Remember, the important thing is that, though it may change, even momentarily, you should still always be doing your number one priority. Generally it will be the activity you have listed. It will most likely not be any of the number of other activities further down on your list.

How many times at the end of a day have you said, "I didn't get anything done today"? How much better would it be to be able to say, "All I got done today was my number one priority"? When you finish number one, you go on to number two, which has then become number one.

Roll With the Benefits

Many helpful ideas on managing your time are included in my husband's book *Managing Yourself,* and in other books named in the Resource List. But let me share just one more idea. I'm a very scheduled person. I find it easy to arrange my time according to these principles. However, with my small children, I have found that many times the day just hasn't gone the way I planned. I had scheduled something during naptime or while the children were being cared for, but then one of them didn't sleep, or one of them got sick, or a babysitter wasn't available. I found it extremely frustrating not to accomplish what I had planned. Sometimes I would flex and find other things to do. Often, though, my frustration level would grow, and at the end of the day I would throw up my hands and say, "I just can't get anything done!"

From that frustration came an approach to my schedule that has helped me tremendously, not only in accomplishing things with small children, but in a lot of attitudes in my life. I call it, "Rolling with the benefits rather than resisting the situation."

I continue to plan and to schedule. I have some long-term goals for my life and some short-term plans. I have "to do" lists. I know my basic priorities. I even schedule, often in my mind rather than on paper, what I'm going to do during certain periods of time.

The refinement that I have added to this involves knowing what I can do in certain kinds of time blocks. For example, when my children are being cared for by someone else, I can do certain kinds of major, time-consuming, creative things, or I can accomplish things that require uninterrupted time, such as writing, or painting a room. While my children are napping, I can do various shorter-term activities, such as cleaning out a closet, or working on a project that requires some concentration. When one child is awake and another is asleep, I can do things like housework or letter-writing, or I might spend time with the child who is awake. When both of them are awake, I can do still other kinds of things, such as laundry, that require no concentration. When the children require attention, my priority of spending time with them and developing them comes to the forefront.

At first I actually wrote down all the different time blocks I had available and the activities I could do in each, but eventually I had it all in my mind. Then, when something did not occur the way I planned—for example, a child didn't take a nap—rather than be upset because I could not do what I had scheduled, I would shift to something I could do. Knowing what other activities I had and what the priorities were, I knew what I could immediately shift into that time block. Rather than resist a situation I couldn't control, I would roll with the benefits.

My friend Laurie Killingsworth, a busy mother of four, sums up these thoughts so well: "These are useful tools only as our lives are in right order. When we're doing what God wants us to do, He, who is the giver of time, gives us the time to do it. He plans our day, including not providing time for the things He does not want us to do. He delays us, puts us in unusual places we couldn't have planned for, and changes our paths. When something comes up to take our time from our previously planned project, we don't have to feel frustrated, because He's in control of our moments just as surely as He's in control of the universe.

"I constantly say, 'Slow me down, Lord.' When I'm running at a fast pace and doing, doing, doing, I often get ahead of the Lord. Too many of us do this and we begin to tackle jobs that the Holy Spirit didn't mean for us to do. Instead of asking the Lord what He wants to bless, we ask Him to bless what we have started."

Managing Your Home

Another big help in being able to minister both to your family and beyond your family is to have your home well managed. My friend, Mary Johnson, who occasionally teaches a class on home management, and who cares for her two boys, suggests a few simple but strategic ideas.

The first thing to do is walk through your home. In each room ask, What is the function of this room? What do we do in this room? What could we do to make this room most effective for its purpose?

The next step is to get rid of clutter. You might have three boxes as you start going through rooms or closets or parts of the house. One is a "throw-away," another is a "give-away," and a third is a "put-away" box. Everything should go into one of those boxes. Those things that go into the put-away box then must be put away. It's vital to have a place for everything—files, book shelves, closets, drawers, the garage.

Another step in getting rid of the clutter is to give all your clothes the one-year test. Have I worn this in the past year? If not, then I ought to get rid of it. Of course, in the baby-bearing years, weight and shape fluctuations necessitate a longer "keep" time.

Next, you need to organize for efficiency. Considering what you do in each room, place things where they are most efficiently used. Make sure you have easy access to things that you use often—keeping them at arm's length and easily removed; don't stack them. Things that are used less often can be in more difficult-to-reach places. Keep your work surfaces as clear and clutter-free as possible. Store things in see-through containers or label them clearly so that you don't have to look through boxes to find something you want.

Include the family in your home organization. This will help build confidence, character and responsibility as well as save you work. Use chore charts or some other way to make sure every person knows what his or her responsibilities are. You need to show children how to do what you want them to do, give them guidelines, and inspect what they've done. Often children don't do what we've asked them to because they really don't know how.

Finally, remember to enjoy your home. I have a friend whose home is immaculate. She has small children, and I'm not sure it's possible for those children to enjoy the home.

It's good to put things away right after they're used, but to be rigid and not allow a child to change what she's doing and to enjoy herself doesn't allow the home to be a comfortable place. Do your guests feel relaxed when they visit? Does your husband feel at ease when he comes home? I find that for most people a balance between neatness, order and lack of clutter, and a sense that we can live here and do things in this home, seems to be the best. People are important.

Several helpful books on home management are included in the Resource List.

Child Care

Another area of need for many mothers is child care. Although you will undoubtedly include your children in your ministry often and certainly you will seek to minister from your home, at times the ministry to which God has called you will require that someone else care for your children.

One of the most obvious means of child care is the church children's program. When you are ministering through or during a church activity time, care for children is almost always available.

Another common child-care arrangement is to trade with a friend or a neighbor. Some do this occasionally and others do it on a regular basis, say once a week. I have friends who have established a weekly evening child-care co-op. Once a month they have the care of four families' children, but for the other three weeks they have one night each week to themselves.

Sometimes friends or teenagers are sympathetic to what you are doing and consider it a ministry to care for your children while you are involved.

Grandparents are a wonderful alternative. I feel so privileged that Steve's mother moved near us and loves to care for our children—and they love to be with her. When grandparents aren't available, perhaps elderly neighbors or church members could become like grandparents. You, your children, and the adopted "grandparents" all can benefit in important ways from this.

Bible study groups sometimes have someone care for all the children in one home while the Bible study is taking place in another.

Many churches provide "Mother's Day Out" programs. This gives your child a regular, comfortable place to go.

Some of my friends and I have found several single women and even some single men who love to be included in the lives of children. They gladly baby-sit or take the children on outings or get involved in their lives in other ways. This gives the children other models, and it gives our single friends interaction and time with the children and with a family. And, of course, it can be of great help to you when you need time for reaching out.

Hiring baby sitters is another option. One family has a college girl from their church living with them. They are able to minister to her as she is a part of the family, and she is able, on occasion, to provide child care when it's needed.

Another family reports taking a high school or college girl on trips with them. She helps with the children while the parents are involved in ministry, yet the children still get to be included in the outreach, and so does their companion.

When you must be gone for more than a day, it is good to leave the children with someone who has children with whom yours play regularly so they are comfortable and don't feel lost. Also helpful for these short trips would be to have a couple without children stay in your home. Your children will enjoy the attention, and it could be helpful for the couple as they look toward having their own family someday.

Of course, the most ideal child care for you in your ministry is for Dad to spend the time with the children. My husband is very good at encouraging my ministry time by caring for Debbie and Michelle, often making it a special fun time.

These ideas for time scheduling, home management and child care all can provide significant help in discovering and stepping into God's ministry opportunities for you. However, God Himself provides the most significant help of all.

17
The Power Source

So you've committed yourself to ministry. You want to be available to step into God's opportunities to touch lives for Him. You've chosen an area of ministry to your family and beyond your family. You're ready for God to use you!

Stop! Before you go any further, you must make sure you have appropriated the most important resource of all—the power of God.

Even as ministry is to be true for every child of God, so are we to draw on God's power for accomplishing the ministries He gives us. We cannot perform any ministry by ourselves. We cannot lead people to Christ. We cannot help people in our own strength. The power for effective ministry comes from God the Father pouring out His power in our lives through His Holy Spirit indwelling and filling us.

Where the Power Comes From

Two things are essential if we are to experience that power. The first is to understand the source. As we mentioned earlier, a supernatural life is one that is lived moment by moment in the power of the controlling Spirit of God.

Every child of God—each one of us who has received Christ as Savior—has been indwelt by the Holy Spirit. The Holy Spirit has come to live in us. But not every one of us is filled and empowered by the Holy Spirit.

161

If there's no power in our lives, if there is lack of faith, if there is disobedience, if worry and discouragement and frustration characterize our lives, then we are not filled with the Spirit of God.

God has promised so much to us when we allow Him to fill us and control us every moment. He promised in Acts 1:8 that "you will receive power when the Holy Spirit comes on you; and you will be my witnesses in Jerusalem, and in all Judea and Samaria, and to the ends of the earth." He tells us that the fruit of the Spirit—the natural result of allowing Him to control our lives—is love, joy, peace, patience, kindness, goodness, faithfulness, gentleness, self-control (Galatians 5:22,23). And the Spirit filling us gives us power for our daily lives—to cope with circumstances, to experience the abundant life, to live in victory, not defeat (John 10:10; Romans 8:37).

When we are filled with God's Spirit by faith, we can experience the abundant and fruitful life which Christ has promised to each Christian. In Ephesians 5:18 we are commanded: "Do not get drunk on wine, which leads to debauchery. Instead, be filled with the Spirit." And in 1 John 5:14,15 we have this promise: "If we ask anything according to his will, he hears us. And if we know that he hears us—whatever we ask—we know that we have what we asked of him."

Prayer of Faith

We are filled with the Holy Spirit by faith, and prayer is one way of expressing faith. You can make sure, right now, that you are filled and controlled by the Spirit of God. You might pray something like this, if it expresses the desire of your heart:

"Dear Father, I need You. I acknowledge that I have been in control of my life, and that, as a result, I have sinned against You. I thank You for forgiving my sins through Christ's death on the cross for me. I now invite Christ to again take control of my life. Fill me with the

Holy Spirit as You commanded me to be filled and as You promised in Your Word that You would do if I asked in faith. I pray this in the name of Jesus. As an expression of my faith, I thank You for taking control of my life and for filling me with Your Holy Spirit."

If by faith you have appropriated the power of God's Spirit in your life, you can be sure that you are filled with His Spirit. Do not depend on feelings. The promise of God's Word, not our feelings, is our authority. We must live by faith, that is, trust, in the trustworthiness of God Himself and His Word.

But what if you become aware of an area of your life—an attitude or an action—that is displeasing to the Lord, even though you are walking with Him and sincerely desiring to serve Him? Simply thank God that He has forgiven your sins—past, present and future—on the basis of Christ's death on the cross. Claim His love and forgiveness by faith and continue to have fellowship with Him.

If you retake control of your life through sin—a definite act of disobedience—then you need to breathe spiritually. Spiritual breathing is an exercise in faith. It enables you to continue to experience God's love and forgiveness.

1. Exhale. Confess your sins. Agree with God concerning your sin and thank Him for His forgiveness of it, according to 1 John 1:9 and Hebrews 10:1-25. Confession involves repentance—a change in attitude and action.

2. Inhale. Surrender the control of your life to Christ and appropriate—receive—the fullness of the Holy Spirit by faith. Trust that He now controls you and empowers you according to His command in Ephesians 5:18 and the promise of 1 John 5:14,15. (See the booklet "Have You Made the Wonderful Discovery of the Spirit-filled Life?")

A Vital Walk

The second essential thing for consistently drawing on

God's power — and one of the most difficult areas for
mothers with young children — is to maintain a vital walk
with God through study and fellowship and prayer. Most
mothers have struggled with this, and some have discovered some ways to keep that freshness in their
relationship with God.

Donna Lynn: My greatest help in maintaining my
time and walk with God is to escape the stereotype of
"just me and a Bible or it doesn't count." God under-
stands my need for Him and is always creative in helping
me to spend time in my mind with Him when He knows
I really want to. My day turns into a constant prayer and
praise time.

When I play Christian music, it brings music and
praise to my young child. Tape recordings of the Scripture provide company for my child as well as time in the
Word for me. When I take my child on a stroll around the
block, I point out a tree and thank God for trees. I talk
with my children about people for whom we're thankful,
and we thank God for them. I read my Bible while nursing an infant. The Bible stories I read to my children I
relive and apply to myself. I have verses above the
kitchen sink and on the bathroom wall. As I watch my
children run and jump, I praise God for their healthy
bodies. And I always have a little time alone with Him at
bedtime or early in the morning.

Kathy: I jog regularly and I make sure that I use that
time for praise and prayer rather than for thinking on
other things of the day. It's almost impossible to be interrupted while jogging. And just being outside gets me
in the mood for prayer.

Barbara: Riding in the car is great for time with the
Lord. I also find that not getting my hopes up for big
chunks of time is helpful. I trust that if I get only five or
ten minutes with Him, He'll make it good. My biggest
problem is choosing to actually stop and meet with Him
when the opportunity comes.

Carol: I have had to recognize that even a short time
with the Lord is better than none. I find using an induc-

tive study guide most helpful because it makes me think and apply the Word personally and is easy to pick up where I've left off.

Molly: For me, rising in the morning before the rest of the family is the best thing to do.

Pamela: Writing out my devotions has helped me. No matter how often I am interrupted, I can come back to the place where I left off. I've also had to unlearn the Christian myth about the time, place and frequency of devotions. Christian radio, records and tapes are important.

Coryne: When my children were small, my husband cared for them once a month for half a day while I had a time with the Lord. Other than that I planned my quiet times around the children's nap times. I tried to set aside time before bed to read.

Judy: I found that taking teaching or discipling responsibilities forced me to prepare and to study. I also found discussing questions with my husband was helpful. I learn a lot from him. I analyzed how I learn best and realized that two or three longer segments of time each week were better than trying to have daily study times.

Probably the most helpful idea for me is to listen to Scripture tapes. I often did that while nursing babies. And even now Steve and I keep a tape recorder and Scripture tapes in the bathroom. Each morning as we get ready for the day, we fill our minds with God's Word.

Perhaps one of these ideas would be just right to help you maintain that warm and vital relationship with your heavenly Father.

As you live a supernatural life, as you walk moment by moment in the power of God's Holy Spirit, as you maintain that vital, fresh, constant relationship with a loving God, be assured that He will lead you to opportunities to minister, to reach out, to touch a life for Him.

18
Yes, a Mother Can!

So, what can a mother do? Is there a balance? Is it possible to minister to your family as God has called you to, to give unselfishly to them and help them grow into the people God intends for them to be, and at the same time to reach beyond your family and minister to others, to be available to God to step into an opportunity to touch a life for Him?

Mothers in the Midst

Listen to what some mothers in the midst of discovering that balance have to say:

> Barbara Brand: I think it is a tragic misconception among mothers that children are a limitation to a dynamic and fruitful ministry. I believe the Scriptures teach that, whatever my role and responsibilities in life, God in His wisdom has chosen what is integral to my becoming conformed to the image of Christ. He will equip me for every good work—for a meaningful ministry—no matter where I am. If I have been single for many years or if I have ten children, God is not limited by my situation. I can flourish in it if I have the proper mindset.
>
> For a mother with small children the issue is not how does helping to fulfill the Great Commission fit in with my being a wife and mother with small children, but rather, how does my being a wife and mother with small children fit in to helping to fulfill the Great Commission?

With that perspective we don't limit God on how He wants to and can use us.

Sara Randall: My husband and my daughter are the most precious parts of my life. I feel that everything I do involving either of them is ministry. When God calls us to marriage and then to motherhood, He gives increase in ministry. Marriage and motherhood give enrichment and significance that my life wouldn't otherwise have. But my relationship with the Lord — and His calling to me — overrides everything. So reaching out to the world around me, or as far away as I can go, is not an option. Somehow that has to be going on in my life because I am called of God. I am a child of God and His Scripture applies to me. But nothing in my life is going to work unless my personal walk with God is what it should be.

Diane Hutcheson: When we have had a taste of what it is to walk in the Spirit and reach others for the Lord and begin to disciple them, we will never be satisfied if that is not in our life in some way. It's so easy when we get two or three children, have a busy husband and get comfortable in our home, to be lulled into concentrating on a new house or redecorating or a new aerobics class. But those things won't satisfy.

Certainly there are certain periods in our lives that provide minimal opportunities, but we must always maintain our personal time with the Lord, for that gives us God's viewpoint instead of the world's viewpoint. That keeps me on track, recognizing that God has called me out of the world in order to send me back into the world to have an impact and to experience His heart for the world.

I can't speak for the next person, but in my life I've got to be used, reaching out to somebody or at least on my way seeking to reach somebody. I find myself saying, "Lord, thank You that You have built these desires into my life and that I can never be fully satisfied unless I'm doing what You created me for."

Mothers Who Have Been There

We can learn a lot from mothers who have had a few

more years of experience and have found some of that balance God has for them.

Vonette Bright: I've always felt that God had to be first in my life. Then my responsibility is to my husband, to my children and finally to my ministry. But I have also found that I am a better wife and a better mother when I have some kind of outreach, some way in which I am developing personally. I think the excited Christian is the one who is applying Scripture in her daily life, and to make that application you need to have some means of expressing it. Scripture becomes real not only when you apply it in your own circle to what you are doing, but also as you pass it on to someone else. It then becomes even more valid.

I think there is such great satisfaction in seeing your life being duplicated in the lives of others — your family or someone else. It's so good to see that you are helping to meet a need in the life of another person. At the same time you know you are growing. You know you are letting God be original in helping you develop into the person He wants you to be.

Judy Anderson: The Lord sees my life in its totality. All the parts make one complete unit. Within that perspective my ministry to my husband and my children has priority. Obedience, satisfaction and fruitfulness in this area provide a good foundation for reaching out to others.

For I do have a responsibility to the Great Commission — to reach non-Christians, and to disciple those who receive Christ as well as other Christians. I believe exercising my spiritual gifts will also involve me in other people's lives. I must be an example to my children and so help to form in them a heart of compassion for the spiritual and material needs of others. My life is kept in better perspective and less egocentric when I am involved in reaching out to others.

I would tell young mothers to expect the years of motherhood to be rich, and to anticipate daily joy and blessing because of your children. But don't limit your view of what you can do. Understand yourself, and be open to whatever the Lord may want for you, how He may change you and what He will produce through you.

Pamela Heim: It's so important to have a sense of who I am. I am valued by God. I have a worth. He has created me and He wants to do a unique, original thing through me. I need to understand my giftedness, my part in the body of Christ. But I think there are times when you're home with your children that God somewhat puts aside your gifts in order to develop your character. Think of Joseph and all he went through before he became second in command in Egypt. And think of Moses' forty years in Pharaoh's court and forty years herding sheep before he was prepared to do the ministry God had for him. So, relax. Enjoy these years. Don't take on unnecessary pressures about becoming all you need to become in one decade of your life.

If we are committed to serving Jesus Christ, to being His person, there is a beautiful relaxation in that. We only have to be the person God wants us to be at any one point in history. I don't always have to be trying to figure out what I can do next to serve God. He knows my heart, and He knows that when He opens doors, I'm going to walk through them. The interesting thing to me is that, as He has opened the doors, they have always fit very well with where my family is at that point.

Donna Lynn Poland: My family is my number one priority and all other opportunities must take my husband and children into consideration. If I minister to my husband and children with the wholehearted commitment God wants me to, my outreach will include what God does through their lives as well—multiplication with the greatest possibilities.

At different times in a mother's life she may feel she has no "special ministry" due to circumstances inside the home. The need to pull back and re-evaluate is a constant possibility, depending on the fluctuating needs of husband and children. I must constantly be willing to give up whatever I need to in order to keep family the priority they should be. But I will find many natural opportunities always waiting. It's often not until we're willing to give up the stereotyped idea of "ministry" outside the home that God shows us the creative natural opportunities for touching lives for Him.

I would encourage every mother to submit her will to God to become an unselfish person. This makes parenting much easier, to say nothing of the glory it brings to God because of our character growth. Doggedly pursue your relationship with God. Without constant vigilance for time in the Word, constant praying, listening to God, learning through our children and the experiences of life, feedback from our husbands and others, we'll not make it. Humanly, it is impossible to be a good parent. Don't try it on your own strength. The Spirit-filled life is the only way.

Remember that children are children such a short time. Get yourself together so you can spend these years enjoying them, teaching them, shaping them, giving them joy, ministering with them and not trying to figure out how you can get away from them to fulfill your needs and live your life.

Principles for Life

As I seek to discover God's balance for me, I find it's useful to have some guiding principles, some steady reference points to help me sort out the possibilities and opportunities. Let me share five such life principles with you.

First, *keep your life goals before you.* Know where you are going and how you expect to move in that direction. Look at these goals often so they will help you make the right choices for the right day.

Second, *remember you are a significant person.* God made you in His image. God loves you so much He sent His Son, Jesus Christ, to die for you. God has a wonderful, specific plan for your life. When you don't feel significant, when you don't seem to be accomplishing very much, when mothering seems so tedious, remember you are significant and God will use you in a significant way.

Third, *recognize that home is the most important place in the world.* What happens in our home determines the future of our children and our world. Home is where our children must gain the strength, security, confidence, affirmation and love they need to go out into the world and be and do all that God has for them.

Fourth, *realize that you have something significant to contribute to your family and beyond your family.* God put you in your family. You are the right wife for your husband, the right mother for your children. Just as they will have an impact on your life, so you will influence them significantly. God put you in your neighborhood. He gave you specific skills and abilities and gifts. He has given you certain friends. He gives you definite opportunities. He has meaningful ways for you to contribute.

Finally—and this is most important of all—*do what God wants you to do.* Seek Him above all else. He is more important than all the activities, all the opportunities, all the needs of life. He must be first in our lives. I truly believe that, if we want with all our hearts what God has for us, and if we're willing to do it no matter what it is, He won't let us miss it. The one question that I ask whenever someone is making a difficult decision is, "What does God want you to do?"

Take That Step

Is ministry just for professionals? Is it really for mothers? Surely it is! Every child of God is called to live a supernatural life, to reach out, to minister in the name of Christ.

What opportunities has God given you to step into? Perhaps it will be a more formal opportunity: an outreach within your church, or leading a Bible study, or teaching a children's group. But certainly there also will be the informal opportunities: the lonely neighbor down the street, a young mother whose husband has just left her, the child at home by herself every afternoon, the pregnant teenager, an injustice in your community.

What needs do you see around you that God would want to meet? What do you have that God might use to meet those needs? It might be time, or money, or a listening ear, or a skill, or food, or counsel, or a warm home. But most important, you have Jesus Christ, the one who will ultimately meet all needs.

I never cease to be in awe that God chooses to use me to touch lives for Him. What a privilege and what a responsibility! Yet too often I settle for less than God's best. I'm not available, or I'm too busy with my plans—and I miss God's opportunity for me.

God wants to use you, too. His Word says that He has already prepared good works for you to do (Ephesians 2:10). He has appointed you to bear fruit for Him (John 15:16).

He will give you a supernatural life and supernatural power to do what He wants you to do. He has a ministry just for you. Don't settle for less than God's best. Be open. Be available. And step into the opportunities He provides.

Appendix A
Resource List

MISCELLANEOUS HELP FOR MOMS

Barnes, Marilyn Gwaltney. *Love (and Baby Powder) Covers All*. San Bernardino, CA: Here's Life Publishers, 1984.

Birkey, Verna and Turnquist, Jeanette. *Building Happy Memories and Family Traditions*. Old Tappan, NJ: Revell, 1980.

Bock, Lois and Working, Miji. *Happiness Is a Family Time Together*. Old Tappan, NJ: Revell, 1975.

Bombeck, Erma. *Motherhood — the Second Oldest Profession*. New York: McGraw Hill, 1983.

Bright, Vonette Zachary. *For Such A Time as This*. Old Tappan, NJ: Revell, 1976.

Dillow, Linda and Arp, Claudia. *Sanity in the Summertime — creative ideas and plans for the 90 days when school is out*. Nashville, TN: Thomas Nelson, 1981.

Gaither, Gloria and Dobson, Shirley. *Let's Make a Memory*. Nashville, TN: Thomas Nelson, 1986.

Hancock, Maxine. *People in Process — The Preschool Years*. Old Tappan, NJ: Revell, 1978.

Hunter, Brenda. *Where Have All the Mothers Gone?* Grand Rapids, MI: Zondervan, 1982.

Kelly, Marguerite and Parsons, Elia. *The Mother's Almanac — loving and living with small children*. Garden City, NY: Doubleday, 1975.

Kuzma, Kay. *Prime-time Parenting — how to create quality time with your children*. New York: Rawson, Wade, 1980.

McGinnis, Marilyn. *Give Me a Child Until He's Two (then you take him until he's four!)*. Ventura, CA: Regal, 1981.

Miller, Kathy Collard. *When Love Becomes Anger*. San Bernardino, CA: Here's Life Publishers, 1985.

Owen, Pat Hershey. *The Idea Book for Mothers — how to make your home a fun place to live*. Wheaton, IL: Tyndale, 1982.

Pride, Mary. *The Way Home*. Westchester, IL: Crossway Books, 1985.

Rainey, Dennis and Barbara. *Building Your Mate's Self-Esteem*. San Bernardino, CA: Here's Life Publishers, 1986.

Schaeffer, Edith. *What Is a Family?* Old Tappan, NJ: Revell, 1975.

Schuller, Arvella. *The Positive Family — possibility thinking in the Christian home*. Garden City, NY: Doubleday Galilee, 1982.

Smalley, Gary and Trent, John. *The Blessing.* Nashville, TN: Thomas Nelson, 1986.

Vann, Roger and Donna. *Secrets of a Growing Marriage.* San Bernardino, CA: Here's Life Publishers, 1985.

CHILD DEVELOPMENT

Chapin, Alice. *Building Your Child's Faith.* San Bernardino, CA: Here's Life Publishers, 1983.

Clabby, John F. and Elias, Maurice J. *Teach Your Child Decision Making.* Garden City, NY: Doubleday, 1986.

Coriell, Ron and Rebekah. *A Child's Book of Character Building.* Old Tappan, NJ: Revell, 1980.

Cornell, Joseph. *Sharing Nature with Children.* Nevada City, CA: Ananda Publications, 1979.

Dobson, James. *Dare to Discipline.* Wheaton, IL: Tyndale, 1970.

_____. *Hide or Seek — how to build self-esteem in your child.* Old Tappan, NJ: Revell, 1974.

_____. *The Strong-Willed Child.* Wheaton, IL: Tyndale, 1979.

Fleming, Jean. *A Mother's Heart.* Colorado Springs, CO: Navpress, 1982.

Gibson, Eva. *Intimate Moments.* San Bernardino, CA: Here's Life Publishers, 1986.

Henrichsen, Walter. *How to Disciple Your Children.* Wheaton, IL: Victor, 1981.

Hunt, Gladys. *Honey For A Child's Heart.* Grand Rapids, MI: Zondervan, 1969.

Kuzma, Kay and Kuzma, Jan. *Building Character.* Mountain View, CA: Pacific Press, 1979.

Kuzma, Kay. *Filling Your Love Cup.* Redlands, CA: Parent Scene, 1982.

_____. *Living with God's Kids.* Redlands, CA: Parent Scene, 1983.

LeFever, Marlene. *Growing Creative Children — how to help your child listen, enjoy and participate.* Wheaton, IL: Tyndale, 1981.

Macaulay, Susan Schaeffer. *For The Children's Sake — Foundations of Education for Home and School.* Westchester, IL: Crossway Books, 1984.

McKean, Paul and Jeanne, and Bruehl, Maggie. *Leading a Child to Independence.* San Bernardino, CA: Here's Life Publishers, 1986.

Narramore, Bruce. *Parenting with Love and Limits.* Grand Rapids, MI: Zondervan, 1979.

Ortlund, Anne. *Children Are Wet Cement — Make the right impression in their lives.* Old Tappan, NJ: Revell, 1981.

Rasmussen, Bernard. *Character Craft.* (city unknown: Dupli-craft, 1979).

Smalley, Gary. *The Key To Your Child's Heart.* Waco, TX: Word Books, 1984.

White, Burton L. *The First Three Years Of Life.* New York: Avon, 1975.

PERSONAL DEVELOPMENT

Anson, Elva and Liden, Kathie. *Compleat Family Book — practical helps for a busy home.* Chicago: Moody, 1979.

Barnes, Emilie. *More Hours in My Day.* Eugene, OR: Harvest House, 1982.

Bourke, Dale Hanson. *You Can Make Your Dreams Come True.* Old Tappan, NJ: Fleming H. Revell, 1985.

Bright, Bill. *Ten Basic Steps Toward Christian Maturity.* San Bernardino, CA: Here's Life Publishers, 1968.

Douglass, Steve. *Managing Yourself.* San Bernardino, CA: Here's Life Publishers, 1978.

Gabriel, Ginger. *Being a Woman of God.* San Bernardino, CA: Here's Life Publishers, 1984.

Howard, Grant. *Balancing Life's Demands.* Portland, OR: Multnomah Press, 1983.

Jenson, Irving. *Do-It-Yourself Bible Study Guides.* San Bernardino, CA: Here's Life Publishers.

MacDonald, Gordon. *Ordering Your Private World.* Chicago: Moody Press, 1984.

Ortlund, Anne. *Disciplines of the Beautiful Woman.* Waco, TX: Word Books, 1977.

Precept Ministries. *Inductive Bible Study.* Box 23000, Chattanooga, TN 37422.

Purnell, Dick. *Faith: A 31-Day Experiment.* San Bernardino, CA: Here's Life Publishers, 1985.

_____. *Knowing God by His Names: A 31-Day Experiment.* San Bernardino, CA: Here's Life Publishers, 1987.

_____. *Standing Strong In A Godless Culture: A 31-Day Experiment.* San Bernardino, CA: Here's Life Publishers, 1986.

_____. *The 31-Day Experiment: A Personal Experiment In Knowing God.* San Bernardino, CA: Here's Life Publishers, 1984.

MINISTRY HELPS

Ball, Barbara. *Coffeetalk.* San Bernardino, CA: Churches Alive, 1979.

Bright, Bill. *Transferable Concepts for Powerful Living.* San Bernardino, CA: Here's Life Publishers, 1985.

Bright, Vonette. *Prayer and Praise Diary.* San Bernardino, CA: Here's Life Publishers, 1981.

Briscoe, Jill. *Hush! Hush!* Grand Rapids, MI: Zondervan, 1979.

Christenson, Evelyn. *What Happens When God Answers?* Waco, TX: Word, 1986.

_____. *What Happens When Women Pray?* Wheaton, IL: Victor Books/Scripture Press, 1979.

Davis, Ev and Linda. *Prayer for Those Who Influence Your Family.* Prayer Ministry, Campus Crusade for Christ, Arrowhead Springs, CA 92414.

Duewel, Wesley. *Touch the World Through Prayer.* Grand Rapids, MI: Zondervan, 1986.

Eastman, Dick. *The Hour that Changes the World.* Grand Rapids, MI: Baker Book House, 1981.

Fleischmann, Paul, ed. *Discipling the Young Person.* San Bernardino, CA: Here's Life Publishers, 1985.

Hayes, Dan. *Fireseeds of Spiritual Awakening.* San Bernardino, CA: Here's Life Publishers, 1983.

Heim, Pamela Hoover. *The Woman God Can Use.* Denver, CO: Accent Books, 1986.

Hepburn, Daisy. *How to Grow a Women's Minis-Tree.* Ventura, CA: Regal, 1986.

Mainhood, Beth. *Reaching Your World—Disciplemaking For Women.* Colorado Springs, CO: Navpress, 1986.

Mains, Karen. *Open Heart, Open Home.* Elgin, IL: David C. Cook, 1976.

McCloskey, Mark. *Tell It Often—Tell It Well.* San Bernardino, CA: Here's Life Publishers, 1985 .

Mothers of Pre-schoolers (MOPS, Inc.), 11596 West Colfax, Suite 6, Lakewood, CO 80215, (303) 239-6677.

Nichols, Fern. *Moms In Touch.* 14636 Poway Mesa Drive, Poway, CA 92064.

Olsen, Kermit. *First Steps in Prayer.* St. Paul, MN: MacAlester Park Publishing Co., 1979.

Regions Beyond Missionary Union. *Global Prayer Digest.* Frontier Fellowship, 8102 Elberon Ave., Philadelphia, PA 19111.

Schneider, Darlene. *A Birthday Party For Jesus.* San Bernardino, CA: Here's Life Publishers, 1984.

Storm, Kay Marshall. *Helping Women in Crisis.* Grand Rapids, MI: Zondervan, 1986.

Discipleship Bible Study series. San Bernardino, CA: Here's Life Publishers, 1983.

Good News Comic Book. San Bernardino, CA: Here's Life Publishers, 1970.

How to Make a Mark That's Hard to Erase. San Bernardino, CA: Here's Life Publishers, 1983.

TRAINING SESSIONS

Adventures in Discipleship. A 13-week program to help Sunday school members be growing disciples and do the work of ministry. Here's Life Christian Resource Center, Arrowhead Springs 67-00, San Bernardino, CA 92414, (714) 886-5224.

Child Evangelism Fellowship, P.O. Box 348, Warrenton, MO 63383, (314) 456-4321. They offer training sessions on holding weekly Good News Clubs and 5-Day Clubs in the summer.

Christian Education Growth Dynamics. A comprehensive leadership training program where teachers learn how to lead, motivate and encourage growth in their Sunday school classes. Here's Life Christian Resource Center, Arrowhead Springs 67-00, San Bernardino, CA 92414, (714) 886-5224.

Christian Living Seminars. A five-part video series on the Spirit-filled life and how to share your faith. Here's Life, America, P.O. Box 26160, Austin, TX 78755, (512) 458-2111.

CLASS (Christian Leaders and Speakers Seminars). Provides opportunities for all individuals who wish to improve their communication skills and their ability to express themselves clearly whether in conversation or before groups. CLASS, 1814-E Commercenter West, San Bernardino, CA 92408, (714) 888-8665.

Compassionate Woman Program. Compassion International, 3955 Cragwood Dr., P.O. Box 7000, Colorado Springs, CO 80933, 1-800-336-7676. Bible studies, film and devotional guide for becoming compassionate, caring women.

Dawson, Joy. Tapes on Intercession. Box 591, Tujunga, CA 91042.

Hepburn, Daisy. Heritage Ministries, 823 Edinburgh St., San Francisco, CA 94112. Seminars on how to have a women's ministry in a church.

In His Presence. Eight sessions on prayer. Prayer Ministry, Campus Crusade for Christ, Arrowhead Springs 38-00, San Bernardino, CA 92414, (714) 886-5224.

Managing Yourself. Video tape and leader's guide to go along with the book by Steve Douglass. Here's Life Christian Resouce Center, Arrowhead Springs 67-00, San Bernardino, CA 92414, (714) 886-5224.

Appendix B

Steve and Judy Douglass

GUIDING VERSE
> Train up a child in the way he should go,
> even when he is old he will not depart from it
> (Proverbs 22:6, NASB).

"God's way" is both universal — true for every child of God — and unique — specially designed for each individual.

ULTIMATE OBJECTIVES
1. Know, love and obey God
2. Love and respect all people
3. Maintain curiosity about all of life

Deborah — bee — industrious, efficient
   a prophetess — speaks for God, truth
   a judge — discernment, wisdom
   a military leader — bold, courageous

Ann — grace
   Whatever you do, work at it with all your heart, as working for the
      Lord, not for men (Colossians 3:23, NIV).

Michelle — like God
   godly character
   peaceful spirit
   joyful attitude
   loving heart

Elizabeth — consecrated to God
   totally submitted to God
   set apart for service
   > Be imitators of God, therefore, as dearly loved children
   > (Ephesians 5:1, NIV).

I. SPIRITUAL DEVELOPMENT

   A. Understanding need of salvation
      1. Read Bible stories regularly
      2. Explain "as a way of life"
      3. Share individually when appropriate

   B. Understanding who is "on the throne"
      1. Explain concept of lordship
      2. Practice as a way of life
      3. Talk about "who's the boss?"

   C. Vital relationship with God
      1. Talk about Him often
      2. Pray spontaneously, regularly
      3. Share what we do, why, pray about it
      4. Relate life events, decisions to God, His character
      5. Praise God often
      6. Talk about God's sovereignty
      7. Talk about appropriating God's power

   D. Commitment to prayer
      1. Pray at bedtime
      2. Pray at meals
      3. Pray about needs, thanks
      4. Pray spontaneously
      5. Pray about the day's activities

   E. Familiarity with Scripture
      1. Read as a family
      2. Model reading, studying, applying
      3. Talk about what God says relative to any situation
      4. Memorize
         a. One verse each week by alphabet
         b. Review child care verses
         c. Review Sunday school verses

   F. Ministering to others
      1. Include Debbie and Michelle in our ministry when possible (pray for and go)
      2. Tell them about our ministry opportunities (e.g., celebrating with the angels)
      3. Begin to help them minister to their friends (find a need and fill it)

   G. Commitment to church
      1. Model it
      2. Take them regularly
      3. Talk about it

II. CHARACTER DEVELOPMENT

A. In general
   1. Praise right actions, attitudes
   2. Model right actions, attitudes
   3. Talk about good, bad character qualities as a way of life
   4. Read stories that model positive qualities and discuss them
   5. Pose "what would you do if and why" situations

B. Responsibilities
   1. Give regular responsibilities
   2. Use responsibilities chart each day
   3. Emphasize value of work (in them and us)

C. Honesty/Integrity (esp. Michelle)
   1. Reward honesty in difficult situations
   2. Firmly discipline dishonesty
   3. Encourage an intense concern for righteousness without undue introspection

D. Courage (esp. Debbie)
   1. Seek to provide one new experience or activity each week (teaches lifetime learning attitudes as well)
   2. Encourage them to try new skills or enter new experiences as they arise
   3. Deal with fears lovingly, firmly — let them talk about them

E. Leadership (esp. Debbie)
   1. Provide opportunities to play with older and younger children
   2. Enlist help with other children
   3. Play games, e.g., follow the leader, that give leadership opportunities
   4. Provide opportunities to decide family activities

F. Fruit of the Spirit (esp. Michelle)
   1. Model daily
   2. Encourage loving others in our actions
   3. Practice kindness
   4. Be joyful — play the "happy game"
   5. Smile often
   6. Cast cares on God

G. Humility
   1. Help them learn to say "I'm sorry" willingly and honestly (repentently)
   2. Praise only those things they have accomplished, not what God has given them
   3. Point out all that God has given them — frequently

4. Help them see good qualities in others

H. Generosity
   1. Make and give Christmas and birthday gifts for special people
   2. Share things with each other and with other children
   3. Give things away occasionally, especially to those in need
   4. Make and take things to someone sick or lonely or in need
   5. Give money at church

I. Persistence (esp. Michelle)
   1. Encourage to finish projects, commitments
   2. Provide short-term opportunities for finishing projects

III. SOCIAL DEVELOPMENT

A. Family
   1. Show love, care to each other at all times
   2. Encourage attitude of "I'm for you, we're all for each other"
   3. Time as family once a week
   4. Time alone with Dad, and with Mom, each week
   5. Family day once a month
   6. Give responsibilities so they see they are important family contributors

B. Self-Esteem
   1. Provide opportunities for success
   2. Praise "you did your best"
   3. Shower with unconditional love, acceptance
   4. Criticize actions, not the person

C. Response to authority
   1. Establish clear guidelines and discipline firmly, consistently
   2. Teach that God says obedience is very important
   3. Give examples of results of disobedience as a way of life
   4. Read stories that teach importance of obedience, respect for authority
   5. Teach basic traffic, safety rules as a way of life

D. Relating to others
   1. Model love, respect for others
   2. Emphasize the Golden Rule—help them understand how it works
   3. Provide opportunities for them to relate to people of all ages, different backgrounds and circumstances
   4. Teach good manners
      a. Read stories
      b. Practice with games
      c. Encourage "ma'am" and "sir"

        d. Praise kindness, helpfulness
        e. Provide opportunities to serve

  E. Sense of humor
     1. Laugh a lot
     2. Look for and point out the humorous side of situations
     3. Do fun and funny things
     4. Joke and tease positively

  F. Home skills
     1. Teach them to set and clear the table
     2. Help them learn to clean, cook and wash, and give them
       opportunities to do them
     3. Provide appropriate toys

  G. Proper caution
     1. Teach that God is the ultimate protector
     2. Help to learn discernment on whom to trust, who needs to
       prove who they are
     3. Practice proper responses to various situations

  H. Learning from others
     1. Look at all situations, relationships as opportunities to
       learn and grow
     2. Encourage exposure to and relationships with a variety
       of people

IV. INTELLECTUAL DEVELOPMENT

  A. Reading
     1. Read as often as possible
     2. Respond positively to requests
     3. Always give at least one book at Christmas and birthdays
     4. Provide a variety of books
       a. Classics
       b. Newcomers
       c. Christian
       d. Secular
       e. Teaching
       f. Entertaining
       g. Prose
       h. Verse
       i. Magazines
     5. Visit the library every two weeks
     6. Help them learn to read
       a. Feature different letters w/alphabet cards, verses
       b. Display words/pictures beginning with featured letter
       c. Provide workbooks that teach reading skills
     7. Use the computer

B. Math
 1. Read counting books, encourage them to count
 2. Count and do simple addition and subtraction exercises as a way of life
 3. Play math games
   a. Cuisennaire rods
   b. Pegs
 4. Use the computer

C. Writing
 1. Encourage them to write the featured letter
 2. Use workbooks
 3. Help them learn to write

D. Thinking
 1. Ask them "why" and "how" questions
 2. Help them think through logical results, consequences of various actions
 3. Answer questions with "Why do you think?" etc.
 4. Set up "What if?" situations to discuss
 5. Think aloud as a family as a way of life. Discuss ideas frequently. Icorporate the basics of observation, interpretation, conceptualization (how things relate)

E. General knowledge
   Expose to many situations, things, places, people

F. *Making the Most of Your Mind, Get Better Grades*
   Review periodically for ideas

V. CREATIVE DEVELOPMENT

A. In general
 1. Provide materials
 2. Encourage play
 3. Do at least one creative activity with them each week
 4. Praise all efforts—be as specific as possible
 5. Expose them to different kinds of creative expression
   a. Movie
   b. Ballet
   c. Good music
   d. Art
   e. Museums
   f. Books
   g. Nature walks
   h. Zoo
   i. Disneyland
 6. Emphasize that God the creator makes us creative

7. Help to recognize and go beyond existing limits, boundaries, without losing respect

B. Make-believe/pretend
   1. Provide dress-up clothes
   2. Provide appropriate toys
      a. Dolls/equipment
      b. Animals
      c. Household equipment
      d. Vocational toys
      e. Boxes
   3. Play with them
   4. Encourage fantasies, make-believe friends, made-up games

C. Writing
   1. Have them dictate books
   2. Have them dictate letters
   3. Use the computer
   4. Provide plenty of paper, pencils

D. Art
   1. Provide paper, crayons, markers, paints, books, paste, scissors, clay, junk, old magazines, catalogs
   2. Encourage use of various materials
   3. Help them experiment with different materials, emphasize free expression
   4. Let child care and Sunday school provide opportunities to make "crafts"

E. Music
   1. Provide a variety of records and tapes
      a. Christian children's
      b. Classical
      c. Fun children's
   2. Encourage them to listen to music, talk about it
   3. Take them to musical events
   4. Provide dance, singing opportunities

VI. PHYSICAL DEVELOPMENT

A. Encourage physical activity
B. Seek to develop coordination
   1. Bicycle
   2. Playground equipment
   3. Balls
   4. Tumbling class
   5. Climbing

    C. Seek to develop strength
       1. Trampoline
       2. Playground, esp. monkey bars
       3. Climbing
       4. Hiking

    D. Help gain new skills
       1. Small motor
         a. Practice snapping, buttoning, hooking
         b. Learn to tie a bow
       2. Large motor
         a. Bicycle
         b. Swimming
         c. Ball

    E. Begin to motivate toward athletic interests
       1. Jogging—take them with us occasionally
       2. Tennis
       3. Soccer

    F. Encourage good nutrition
       1. Provide balanced meals
       2. Provide nutritious snacks
       3. Allow only occasional sweets
       4. Explain why we eat what we do and what is wrong with junk food
       5. Don't eat out too often

    G. Encourage safety in all activities
       1. Don't try dangerous things
       2. Be alert
       3. Watch for snakes (we live in the mountains)

VII. FINANCIAL UNDERSTANDING

    A. Teach good stewardship
       1. Encourage saving
       2. Have them use their money occasionally to purchase desired items
       3. Discuss why we can't afford some things, why we don't waste money or things
       4. Encourage giving

    B. Teach the meaning of money
       1. Explain value of different coins, bills
       2. Get an appropriate game
       3. Play store

VIII. PERSONAL HERITAGE

    A. Roots
        1. Expose to cultural, geographic heritage
        2. Encourage appreciation, not pride or prejudice

    B. Memories and traditions
        1. Insure many memorable events
        2. Use photo albums, baby books to record memorable events
        3. Establish family traditions
        4. Maintain blessings book

    C. Lessons learned
        1. Expose to our messages
        2. Encourage to read our articles, books

IX. GENERAL PRINCIPLES

    A. Encourage total God orientation

    B. Be good stewards of our children
        1. Build on strengths
        2. Develop and compensate in areas of weakness

    C. Focus for maximum effectiveness

    D. Occasionally review distilled principles of life (Larry Poland, Shirley Hinkson, Bobb Biehl, Bill and Vonette Bright)

Notes

Chapter One

1. Bruce Narramore, *Parenting with Love and Limits* (Grand Rapids, MI: Zondervan, 1979), p. 111.

Chapter Three

1. Dr. Jack Raskin, quoted by Dale Mills in "To Work or Not to Work After the Baby Comes," *Seattle Times Magazine* (July 1, 1979), p. 8.

2. Dr. Urie Bronfenbrenner, quoted by Susan Byrne in "Nobody Home: The Erosion of the American Family," *Psychology Today* (May 1977), p. 45.

3. Brenda Hunter, *Where Have All the Mothers Gone?* (Grand Rapids, MI: Zondervan, 1982), p. 93.

4. Burton White, *The First Three Years of Life* (Englewood Cliffs, NJ: Prentice Hall, 1975).

5. Herbert Orral, quoted by Hunter, *Where Have All the Mothers Gone?*, p. 82.

6. Hunter, *Where Have All the Mothers Gone?*, p. 83.

7. Edith Schaeffer, *What Is a Family?* (Old Tappan, NJ: Revell, 1975), p. 47.

Chapter Four

1. Maurice Sendak, *Where the Wild Things Are* (New York: Harper & Row, Junior Books, 1984), n.p.

2. Tom Allen, "When Mothers Work," *Worldwide Challenge* (July/August, 1985), p. 37.

3. Margaret Albrecht, *Complete Guide for the Working Mother* (Garden City, NY: Doubleday and Co., Inc., 1967), p. 167.

4. *101 Practical Ways to Make Money at Home* (New York: Good Housekeeping Books), p. 2.

5. *101 Practical Ways*, p. 11.

6. Interview with Deborah Fallows, *U.S. News and World Report* (February 24, 1986).

7. Mary Pride, *The Way Home* (Westchester, IL: Crossway Books, 1985) p. 132.

8. Pride, *The Way Home*, pp. 164-66.

Chapter Five

1. Judy Downs Douglass, "Blending Family Life and on the Road Ministry: An Interview with Josh and Dottie McDowell," *Family Life Today* (July 1983), p. 44.

2. Kay and Jan Kuzma, *Building Character* (Mt. View, CA: Pacific Press, 1979), p. 143.